ADVANCED
RETRIEVER
TRAINING

ADVANCED
RETRIEVER
TRAINING

Laura Hill

The Crowood Press

First published in 2020 by
The Crowood Press Ltd
Ramsbury, Marlborough
Wiltshire SN8 2HR

enquiries@crowood.com

www.crowood.com

This impression 2021

British Library Cataloguing-in-Publication Data
A catalogue record for this book is available from the British Library.

ISBN 978 1 78500 755 2

Cover photograph: Pip Wheatcroft
Frontispiece: Linda Grinham

Typeset by Derek Doyle & Associates, Shaw Heath

Printed and bound in India by Replika Press Pvt. Ltd.

CONTENTS

ACKNOWLEDGEMENTS

First and foremost, I have to thank my parents who gave me such a fulfilled childhood and start in life, which made possible all the things that I have achieved since. Their love and support for everything that I have done has been unwavering.

I am indebted to two special gundog mentors: the late Dave Probert, who was instrumental in giving me sound and practical advice from the beginning, and Guy Bennett, who helped me in later years to develop my own style and methods, and who has continued to give invaluable advice with troubleshooting. I am thankful, too, to all my colleagues and friends who have helped me at various stages. I have learnt so much over the years, as well as laughing and crying plenty along the way. And hopefully there is still more to come.

Next I must thank Karen and Colin Rodger at Bern Pet Foods, who believed in me so early on, and who have been amazing with their long-term nutritional support of my team. Using ACANA has been instrumental in ensuring that my dogs are always in peak physical condition.

A picture is worth a thousand words. I could not have managed without the generous and patient contribution of Pip Wheatcroft, who has provided so many of the photographs and diagrams to illustrate and accompany my text. Other photographers and friends in the gundog world have also kindly contributed their images, including: Gary Barrett, Caroline Bridges, Marie-Eve Buchs, Caroline Dell, Barry Dutton, Patrice Fellows, Linda Grinham, George Howard, Stephen Hunter, John Jeffrey, Vanessa King, Sharon Kitson, Greg Knight, John Lupton, Sarah Middleton, Spencer Morgan, Neil Rice, Nick Ridley, Sam Thatcher, Sarah Winter and Sue Worrall.

Above all, thank you to my wonderful husband Derek for putting up with me and my 'dog habit', being my sounding board and unerring support. Without him, this fascinating journey would never have even begun.

FOREWORD

'Hello, this is Laura Hill. Do you have a black bitch puppy available please?'

'Yes.'

And so the journey began. A journey I have had the great privilege of being part of, albeit from the back seat. Laura named the puppy 'Pru', and three years later she was Field Trial Champion Jobeshill Octavia.

I had met Laura several times, had been training with her occasionally, but didn't know her very well. I kept a litter sister to Pru and so we spent more time together. We went to the same trainers and did much of the same things, but it soon became depressingly obvious that Pru was in a different league. I assumed my dog just didn't 'have it'! But in hindsight, I realize that I was watching the beginning of the talented trainer that Laura was to become.

Her attention to detail was second to none. She would think about and analyse everything she and Pru did together. She would log weaknesses when they occurred, and go back and work on them, explore the reasons why they were occurring, and adjust her training to overcome them. By doing this she began to form an instinctive insight into how a dog thinks.

Understanding the mental process enables her to break down the dog's schooling so that she achieves the maximum out of the partnership. The training has complete clarity to the dog so it succeeds very quickly. There are no pressures of failure or negative consequences to inhibit the dog's understanding of what is being asked of it. Again, the attention to detail is foremost in her methods: everything is broken down into easy-to-assimilate lessons, both for dog and handler. The individual elements are learned and practised and then put together, enabling the dog to have a very positive attitude to all its work. You only have to watch Laura with her own dogs to see how relaxed and happy they are.

Communication is Laura's forte, and she applies her methods not only to her canine pupils, but also to her human ones. She will gently cajole, use her great sense of humour, and in some cases be quite forthright, but she will always ensure that you and your dog learn, and go away understanding so much more than when you arrived.

Laura has been generous to us all by writing this book, sharing her knowledge, and giving us an insight into how she has achieved success. It will be an inspiration to those who want to get the best out of their relationship with their dog, and aspire to improve the effectiveness of their training.

Jane Fairclough, Jobeshill Gundogs,
December 2019

PREFACE

Rapport: A close and harmonious relationship in which the people or groups concerned understand each other's feelings or ideas and communicate well.

Oxford English Dictionary

My early working title for this book was *Lab Rapport*, which I felt summed up my approach to living with and training my own dogs. But my editor rightly pointed out that this title might cause confusion with distributors – indeed, some might think it was about relationships in laboratories! So reluctantly, I agreed to change it. She was correct, of course, and my new title is much more appropriate, in that it simply says what it is. Furthermore it is rightly inclusive of all retriever breeds, and not just the ubiquitous Labrador.

Advanced Retriever Training uses a holistic approach that will help owners think about and enhance their bond with their retriever, improve understanding of how their dog learns, and make training more effective and polished, using techniques that work. In it, I set out to provide a philosophy on living with, and training, your dog – a mindset, if you like. It is a compilation of my experience and knowledge from teaching, competing and handling. I have also brought in my learning from studying animal behaviour, psychology and communications to inform the retriever training process. The book contains supplementary information from areas outside gundog training, which provides additional insight, as well as personal anecdotes and case studies. My aim is to help you to build your understanding and enjoyment of retriever training, and help you to improve the relationship that you have with your dog.

Although my experience is primarily with Labradors, I have trained and judged every retriever breed both here in the UK and throughout Europe. This has given me additional experience of the various breeds, further insight into the distinctive ways they work, and different methods and approaches used in training them. Much of my own personal experience is through training retrievers (and handlers) specifically for competition, but this is just an extra layer of producing an excellent retriever for the field. I also enjoy picking up, beating, and, when time and funds allow, shooting locally on the farms and estates around us.

The very first gundog book I bought was *Retriever Training* by Susan Scales. It helped me get started on my gundog journey, and it now feels a privilege to produce a book that might be regarded as a worthy follow-on book to this and other introductory manuals. *Advanced Retriever Training* doesn't repeat the basic mechanics of retriever training that you will have gleaned from other books or materials. In it, I will not reiterate the elementary commands or handling skills that should already be familiar, except where I have a different approach to them, or where we need to look more critically at elements that are sometimes glossed over.

Some readers may want to enhance their bond with their gundog or develop their understanding of how their dog learns, some may be looking to improve their confidence as handlers, and others may be looking for more beyond – to move their training to the next level, and take those additional steps into competition work. If you want to 'professionalize' your handling and your overall approach to living and working with retrievers, this book will help you get the best from your gundog and also from yourself as a trainer. It will help you make a 'champion' of your dog – whether that is literally, with the aim of training towards achieving Field Trial Champion status, or simply through training to the very highest level – pushing yourself to become a better and more thoughtful trainer.

Part One looks at the background knowledge that will help you to become a more thoughtful and effective trainer. This includes not only analysing the dog in front of you, but also looking at yourself as a pivotal point in the equation, and then in turn at the different ways to approach training. Then in Part Two we will apply that knowledge to inform and empower the retriever training process. We will be working through the strategy and some of the techniques that will be of benefit in training the retriever to a more advanced level.

Our own dogs have enhanced our lives and are now very much our 'way of life'. I hope you enjoy your training journey as much as I have.

INTRODUCTION

We all have dreams. But in order to make dreams come into reality, it takes an awful lot of determination, dedication, self-discipline and effort.
Jesse Owens, athlete

EARLY YEARS

My gundog journey is far from a traditional one, with no family roots or ties to a shooting background. I grew up on a pleasant suburban housing estate near Romsey in Hampshire. Both my parents worked full time, my mum as a school teacher and my dad as an electronics engineer. And whilst I always enjoyed being outside playing, roller-skating, cycling and exploring nature, due to my parents' work commitments I was never allowed any household pets other than a pair of goldfish and some stick insects.

However, my grandparents always had a dog and a cat, and I used to relish my visits to them in rural Sussex, where grandma would take me off on long woodland walks, often foraging for mushrooms and berries, and generally teaching me about life in the country. Grandpa was an estate agent and the cattle auctioneer at Hailsham market. So I think my love of the countryside definitely had its roots with them.

I was fairly academic at school, and as I moved into the sixth form my enjoyment of language and communication began to grow. I took A levels in English Literature, English Language Studies and French, and considered university places reading either Applied Linguistics or Communications. Eventually I decided on a course at Brunel University (in west London), which included work placements giving me practical experience; in 1991 I graduated with a BSc (Hons) in Communication and Information Studies.

After graduating, I worked in central London

Photo: Caroline Bridges

as a trainee in Corporate PR for Guinness PLC, and after a few years moved on to a role in Consumer PR for Viners of Sheffield (also based in London). From there I decided to take a sabbatical to see a bit more of the world, and embarked on a year of independent travel, back-packing around the world, before eventually ending up in Zimbabwe in 1996. There I met my husband, Derek.

OUT IN AFRICA

Derek was born and bred in Zimbabwe, and had always had dogs, owning his first Labrador bitch at the age of eight. She was from working lines, and later Derek went on to breed two litters of his own under the 'Cobber Hill' affix. I really bonded with his two old black Labradors, Sasha and her daughter Tammy. And it wasn't long before we decided that we should have a Labrador of our own.

Phoebe was my very first dog. She was a dual-purpose Labrador, imported from South Africa as a wedding present from Derek's brother, and with her I started to do a bit of competitive obedience, and showed her at a very amateur level. Only later did I find out about a small, keen group of people doing gundog work. So one day I drove into the bush in my open-top Sunbeam Alpine to go and see what went on at a gundog test. I watched in awe as one competitor lined up their dog and sent it away from him (on an unseen retrieve), and my jaw dropped. I thought it was incredible. I wanted to do that, but didn't think I would ever be able to achieve that skill.

The only gundog club in Zimbabwe held occasional meetings at the local vet's house to watch imported videos from the UK, and they would also meet every so often to train or do a test. I remember that on one such occasion I attended my first test as a competitor. It was a cold game test, and I really didn't have much clue of what I was doing. I sent my dog on a blind retrieve into some long grass and just began calling after her 'seek, seek, seek', as this was the hunt command I had picked up. I was still calling nervously as the dog started to emerge from the cover, and the judge piped up behind me: 'I think you'll find she's sought'! Those days were a lot of fun, but I really felt out of my depth without any formal training or structure.

BACK HOME

In 1999, with the political situation deteriorating rapidly in Zimbabwe, we left the country and returned to the UK. Initially living in rented accommodation while we found our feet, it wasn't until 2001 that we were able to think about owning a dog again. Having had a dual-purpose Labrador in Zimbabwe, we looked to find something similar here, and ended up buying a black bitch, Slievemish Turtledove (Gaby), whose dam was a working bitch and whose sire was a show champion. She was the most beautiful looking dog, and very nicely constructed. She had plenty of working ability and a bomb-proof temperament. But she was a challenge to train, lacking the willingness to work as an equal partner.

Gaby definitely had talent, but very much on her own terms! She was strong willed, if not belligerent, and being a novice trainer I was not equipped to deal with her many quirks and weaknesses. She definitely wasn't the easiest dog to train. But I learned a great deal in my struggles to mould her into some sort of working competition dog. She fulfilled a function as a good picking-up dog on our local shoot, and was retired from competition on finally winning an open working test. Her eliminating faults were, however, numerous, and working with her was mostly deeply frustrating. She lived to the ripe old age of nearly seventeen, and is now buried under an apple tree in our garden. Gaby taught me a lot, not least how to have humility!

Subsequent dogs were definitely 'easier', but all came with different challenges, which is part of the fabric of gundog training. Even with similar breeding lines behind them, no two dogs that I have owned since have been the same to train. It is learning how to adapt to each dog's individual learning style, and understanding their motivations and drivers, that is critical to successful training.

Early on we joined Dove Valley and East Midland gundog clubs, where we took part in group

Slievemish Turtledove (Gaby), our first Labrador in the UK, was an enthusiastic worker but proved a challenge to train. (Photo: Nick Ridley)

Early days at local working tests gave us an introduction to competing.

training sessions, and eventually worked our way up to trying working tests. At the time I enjoyed training the dog, and Derek and I took it in turns to handle Gaby at the training classes. But I was far too nervous to actually compete myself, so I would send Derek out with the dog to have a go at the tests, and I would stand cringing on the sidelines as she found new ways to embarrass his efforts. On more than one occasion I remember the judge asking him to call the dog back, to which he would give a pained look and say 'I'm trying', whilst turning puce with blowing his whistle!

My first real mentor into the sport was Dave Probert, a local 'A' panel judge. He ran a popular Wednesday morning training session at a local ground, and here a group of us became 'regulars'. When the ground lease lapsed the group dissolved, which was very sad, as it had become a bit of an institution, with many a lively discussion over coffee afterwards, and a putting of the

world to rights. Whilst Dave's methods might now be considered 'old fashioned', they gave us all a very good grounding in how things could be perceived from a dog's perspective. He was very 'black and white', and this enabled us to think about consistency and getting the basic foundation and obedience work right, in a way that made sense to the dog. I later found out that it is this early work that is critical to success.

After some years I graduated from Dave's, and went on to develop my own style in training, with the help of another mentor, Guy Bennett. I adapted my methods largely as a response to the type of dog that I was breeding, a dog that was more sensitive and biddable in its approach to learning. I will always be grateful to both Dave and Guy, who in very different ways were instrumental in developing my understanding of gundog training.

My next dog after Gaby was a fully working-bred black Labrador bitch called Donnanview

The winning 'Team GB' at the Euro Challenge 2013, where Stauntonvale Story took top retriever.

Floss (Nellie). She was still fairly 'hard-headed' in her approach to her work, but did go on to be my first field trial winner when she and I entered our first novice stake in 2005 and won it. But she lacked the calm temperament needed to trial consistently, and after giving her a couple of additional runs I realized that she was not going to be successful in open stakes.

FOUNDATION BREEDING

The seeds were sown, however, and I soon became 'serious about gundogs'. With more knowledge under my belt, I was careful in my choice for my next Labrador, and I approached a local trainer, Jane Fairclough, who was about to breed from her very consistent field trial winning bitch, Collaroybanks Willow. I was lucky enough to be able to pick a black bitch from her first litter, Jobeshill Octavia (Pru). She was much easier to train, with

Our five Field Trial Champion bitches (left to right): Jobeshill Octavia, Jobeshill Lotta of Stauntonvale, Stauntonvale Fastnet, Stauntonvale Story and Stauntonvale Tic Bean.

Laura handling Field Trial Champion Stauntonvale Moose Milk at the IGL Retriever Championship 2019 at Glenalmond, Scotland. (Photo: John Lupton)

a strong desire to work with me, which came as a bit of a novelty after my experiences with both Gaby and Nellie.

I was methodical in her training, and this paid off, and she went on to become my first Field Trial Champion just three years later, and double qualifying for the IGL Retriever Championship 2009. She was also later selected for the England Gundog Team in 2011 and 2013. Pru's work ethic was phenomenal, and each season Jane used to borrow her back whenever she could to join her picking up team, when I wasn't working her. Picking up with either Jane or myself, Pru did the work of several dogs right through to her eventual retirement in 2017.

In 2008 I registered my own affix, and Stauntonvale Gundogs was officially born. It was in this year that we also acquired Jobeshill Lotta (Bea), again from Jane. This powerful yellow bitch, a half-sister to Pru, went on to become our second Field Trial Champion in 2012, qualifying for the Championship three times in total, and in turn herself produced two more Field Trial Champions for us, her daughters Stauntonvale Fastnet (Aida)

and Stauntonvale Tic Bean (Kitty). Aida qualified for the Championship four times (twice with me and twice with Derek handling), and at the time of writing Kitty has qualified twice, and was a member of the England Gundog Team 2018. As well as these yellow girls from Bea, we also kept a daughter from our first litter from Pru, Stauntonvale Story (Maud), whom in turn I made up to Field Trial Champion in 2015.

In addition, we have two young dogs out of Aida, Stauntonvale Moose Milk (Moose), who double qualified for the Retriever Championship 2019 and is now also a Field Trial Champion, and Stauntonvale Lemon Posset (Sybil), who is an exciting novice prospect. So it's a truly 'family affair'. Unlike many competition kennels, ours is a little different because we mainly keep bitches, whereas the majority of people who compete seriously in field trials run male dogs, which is more practical because they don't come into season or have time off to have pups.

We now own five Field Trial Champion bitches that are all related – two mothers with their three

Derek Hill with Field Trial Champion Stauntonvale Fastnet at the IGL Retriever Championship 2016 at Ampton, Suffolk.

certainly wasn't 'born into it'. From our early forays in Zimbabwe and then England, dabbling in working tests, we then joined a local shoot to learn the ropes and start picking up with our dogs. We also both applied for shotgun licences, and learned to shoot. Derek is now a keen shot, shooting regularly for field trials too, and had the honour of shooting for the IGL Retriever Championship 2018, held at the local Packington estate in Warwickshire. I am still an 'improver' in terms of shooting, as I will always prioritize working the dogs over shooting. But I do enjoy it when I can, and being able to shoot, and understanding shooting, has given me a much more rounded picture of training and judging a dog for the field.

Despite all this, we are well aware that both of us are still relatively 'new kids on the block' compared with some of the sport's stalwarts, who count their experience in decades. I feel grateful to have reached many milestones since setting up my Stauntonvale kennel just over ten years ago, including winning several field trial awards, qualifying for the Retriever Championship more

homebred daughters. This is unusual, and possibly unique, in the history of working retrievers.

A FRESH FACE

With my unorthodox start into dog ownership in general, and particularly into the shooting and gundog scene, some might consider that I am not traditionally qualified to give a full insight into living with the working retriever. I than ten times, being a member of the England Gundog Team, and making up our six Field Trial Champions.

Success has been relatively rapid for us, but by no means accidental. We've worked determinedly, and my background in communications has stood me in good stead, not only through thinking about interaction at the level of the animal, but also in being able to communicate effectively that understanding and learning to others. Combining this experience with a naturally analytical mind has helped me to problem solve and to think 'outside the box' when it comes to training retrievers.

Handlers waiting in the gallery at the IGL Retriever Championship 2018 at Packington, Warwickshire. (Photo: Marie Eve Buchs)

PART ONE: KNOWLEDGE

1 THE THREE PILLARS OF SUCCESS

Breeding, training and feeding are the three crucial building blocks of our kennel. Without the right starting material, you can only go so far. We are constantly trying to improve our breeding, to give us the very best starting material, but you still need the right training. And feeding is important, too – using good quality food that supports the development of muscles, bones and joints at the same time.

Producing a 'champion' gundog is underpinned by these essential elements. If one part is lacking you are never going to have a dog that wins consistently or is outstanding. You might obtain the occasional win or placing, but you will struggle to be successful year in, year out.

Let us look at each element in turn.

BREEDING

> Don't spend time beating on a wall, hoping to transform it into a door.
>
> Coco Chanel, fashion designer

As I shed a few tears in my former mentor Dave Probert's training cabin one day after a particularly frustrating session with Gaby, he turned to me and said: 'You won't get a donkey to win the Derby.' In his typical manner he was being honest and to the point, not unkind. Other less kind sayings also spring to mind, such as: 'You can't make a silk purse out of a sow's ear.'

Gaby was sired by a show champion out of a run-of-the-mill working bitch. In my mind I had perhaps hoped for a genuine 'dual purpose' Labrador from this combination: the best of both worlds. In reality she turned out to be a 'Jack of all trades, master of none'. She was a nicely constructed dog, with a lovely temperament, had plenty of drive and ability, but lacked any desire to work with me as a team. She also had a stack of eliminating faults, although some of these, admittedly, may have been exacerbated by my lack of experience.

Dave's point was a pertinent one: with the best training in the world you will only go as far as the capability of the individual dog. You can try as hard as possible to get the best out of it, but generally there is a ceiling beyond which you won't progress.

To go to the top, you need to have the very best starting material. If you look around in training groups, you will often see a brilliant dog with lots of natural ability that is only being hampered by an inexperienced or inept trainer. Conversely, you may see an established trainer getting the best out of a dog that would be very poor, or at best average, in a less able person's hands. Ultimately, neither of these examples is going to go all the way, but either may make a passable dog to take into a shooting field. But if we want to go further, and strive to do and be the best we can, then we need to look critically at our 'starting material'.

In all types of animal breeding, whether it is for a sport, such as horse racing, or for showing, such as pigeons or dogs, a great deal of time, effort, thought and money goes into breeding programmes.

It is best to do a lot of homework and research

Pedigree Of
FT CH Stauntonvale Moose Milk

Sex: Male
Date of Birth: 31/03/2016
Reg. No.: 3526DC
Breed: Labrador
Colour: Yellow
Breeder: Mrs L Hill
Owner: Mr D Hill
Hips: 5:3
Elbows: 0:0

FT CH Kestrelway Freddie Hips: 2:2 Elbows: 0:0	**FT CH Waterford Fergus** Hips: 4:5 Elbows: 0:0	**FT CH Willowyck Ruff** Hips: 3:4 Elbows: 0:0	FT CH Willowyck Henman	FT CH Pocklea Remus
				Dagleys Girl
			Cleeveway Nestle	FT CH Tasco Dancing Brave of Willowyck
				Sulleys Hill Adder
		FT CH Waterford Covey Hips: 4:2	FT CH Flashmount Socrates	Flashmount Danny
				Zephyr Wisker of Flashmount
			FT CH Crosbyrose Piper of Waterford	FT CH Pocklea Remus
				Mallowdale Dot of Crosbyrose
	Nobsquinton India of Kestrelway Hips: 4:3 Elbows: 0:0	FT CH Mansengreen Diesel of Bridsgreen Hips: 3:3 Elbows: 0:0	Tasco Brimstone	FT CH Letermore Trout
				FT CH Stormwatch Spider of Tasco
			FT CH Shorthorn Ninja of Mansengreen	Millbuies McCoy
				Bringwood Becky
		FT CH Nobsquinton Lily Hips: 8:9	Holbatch Medlar	Wymondham Neptune of Holdgate
				Hobatch Crest
			Princess Thomasina	Brown of Holbatch
				Lady Tiwi
FT CH Stauntonvale Fastnet Hips: 3:3 Elbows: 0:0	**FT CH Eastdale Harry** Hips: 3:7 Elbows: 0:0	**FT CH Greenbriar Viper of Drakeshead** Hips: 7:3 Elbows: 0:0	FT CH Lafayette Tolley	FT CH Kilderkin Renoir
				Black Purdy of Keswick
			Greenbriar Solitaire	FT CH Pocklea Remus
				Fobbingacres Fern of Greenbriar
		Daughting Dulcie of Eastdale Hips: 8:2	Lancaster Bomber	Turramurra Santa of Follybreeze
				Birchams Skylark
			Eastdale Elsa	FT CH Eastdale Danny
				Shadowbrae Star
	FT CH Jobeshill Lotta of Stauntonvale Hips: 4:2 Elbows: 0:0	Tasco Brimstone Hips: 6:3 Elbows: 0:0	FT CH Letermore Trout	FT CH Carnochway Daniel
				Lettermore May
			FT CH Stormwatch Spider of Tasco	Gillmhor Arrow of Pocklea
				Tasco Yellow Belle of Stormwatch
		Collaroybanks Willow Hips: 3:3 Elbows: 0:0	FT CH Craighorn Bracken	FT CH Aughacasla Sam of Drakeshead
				FT CH Lochmuir Bonnie
			Whissendine Barley	FT CH Dargdaffin Dynamo
				Sareen Silver Lady

Produced using PedPro

A breeder pedigree, with Field Trial Champions marked in red.

before selecting a potential breeder and eventually purchasing a puppy to be your new working gundog. More often than not, once you have found the breeder that is right for you, you will have to ask to go on their waiting list for a puppy, as they are likely to be over-subscribed.

So, how do we characterize successful breeding, and what are the key elements to producing the best working dogs? It is not just a case of looking through the pedigrees of potential puppies and picking the ones with the most 'red' in them (Field Trial Champions are traditionally shown in red on breeders' pedigrees). There are some people who seem obsessed with collecting as many champions as possible in a pedigree, without any knowledge of the traits behind them. In turn, there are some breeders who will also put their field trial winners, award winners, or even in some cases working test winners in red too, just to make the pedigree look good to the uninitiated buyer. Interpreting a pedigree can therefore sometimes prove tricky.

It is unlikely that an initial study of a pedigree, or of the parents themselves, will provide an inexperienced puppy buyer with a realistic assessment of the probable inheritance of certain characteristics that they may desire. Without in-depth knowledge of the names in the pedigree, and whether these dogs are known for passing on their traits with any consistency to future generations, it is impossible to interpret potential outcomes accurately.

Good breeders are those who consistently produce superior dogs, time and again, from different couplings. They have a good eye and sometimes some intuition, but more than anything they have a vast knowledge of the working breed and have put a great deal of research and planning into their litters. They are well aware that it is not just the innate qualities or traits of the dog himself (phenotype), but what he is passing on (genotype) or adding to the mix on a variety of dams which is important.

As a potential puppy buyer, you would do better to ask the owners of the sire or dam what the characteristics of any offspring have been, rather than what the parents themselves are like. Obviously this is only possible with older,

seasoned stud dogs or bitches that are on their second or subsequent litter. But it will give you a more rounded picture of the sort of traits that you might be able to expect from your new pup.

OUTCROSSING VERSUS LINEBREEDING

Another thing to bear in mind when looking at pedigrees is the method the breeder has used to put the proposed mating together. This will be either an 'outcross', where the two dogs are totally unrelated, or 'linebreeding', where the parents share some common ancestry. The third method, which we will disregard in this discussion, is inbreeding, which is defined as a breeding of a parent to a son/daughter or a brother to a sister. This is specifically forbidden by the UK Kennel Club.

Let us look at what these breeding methods mean for potential litters. In an outcross, the two dogs are not related, and their combined Coefficient of Inbreeding (COI) is around the breed average, or lower. (You can check this out on the Kennel Club's excellent online MateSelect tool.) For Labradors, the UK COI is currently 6.5 per cent, for Golden Retrievers it is 8.8 per cent, and for Flat Coated Retrievers it is 6.2 per cent. Puppies from an outcross mating will have no common ancestors in the first four lines of their pedigree, and so their pedigree is a mix of two non-related gene pools. This sort of mating brings diversity to the mix. And breeders will periodically outcross to bring 'fresh blood' or new traits into their lines, and to mitigate any faults that are provoked by homozygous recessive genes – that is, cancelling out a negative trait. It can, however, also weaken or diminish positive traits.

The reasons to do an outcross are to bring in a trait or characteristic that was absent in the breeder's lines, and to improve 'vigour' where there has been a demonstrable lack of disease resistance or some infertility in a line. It is thought to be a means to an end by some, and ultimately results in less uniformity in offspring as the genes are more random and diverse.

Linebreeding is a term used to describe a mild form of inbreeding, whereby breeders will choose matings where one or more relatives occur more than once in a pedigree. Jay Lush, a student of Sewall Wright (who devised the coefficient of inbreeding), describes linebreeding as a system that pairs animals that 'are both closely related to the admired ancestor but are little if at all related to each other through any other ancestors.' Lush made an important contribution to the scientific breeding of animals with his book *Animal Breeding Plans* (1937), much of which is still valid for today's breeders.

Thus linebreeding is used to 'set' various traits. With the dogs sharing some common ancestry, breeders have a good idea of what they will get from the mating, and are dealing more with 'known quantities'. Used thoughtfully, breeders can use this method to fix type, temperament, working qualities or structure into their progeny, with parents producing pups of very similar type. The outcome is less random than with outcrossing. Linebreeding is a means for breeders to establish their own lines within the working breed, and a way of fixing in the characteristics they desire most. However, the tighter the breeding, the more likelihood there is of passing on recessive inheritable conditions, too. So there is the potential for doubling up on both good and bad. If line-bred dogs only inherited the best features of their parents, then that would be fine. But of course, it does also increase the risk of genetic defects and hereditary diseases being passed on to future generations.

Reputable breeders are looking to improve the quality of the dogs they breed, whilst also acting as custodians of the breed as a whole.

CONSISTENCY VERSUS DIVERSITY

This provides a dilemma for the thoughtful breeder. Whilst outcrossing is good for the future of the breed as a whole, to maintain genetic diversity, it is not good at improving quality and consistency in particular lines. And whilst linebreeding improves consistency in our progeny, it doesn't contribute in a positive way to the long-term future of our breed.

A moderate approach should be adopted, with both points of view in mind. Trying to improve the overall quality of the animals we produce, whilst all the while having the future of the breed in mind, is what reputable breeders should be striving for. We should try to avoid 'popular sire syndrome' where one dog is used too much because he is fashionable or the winner of the Retriever Championship. The recessive genes he passes on will inevitably meet up again when descendants and half-siblings are mated, and we will breed ourselves into a corner.

Great breeders will know and understand the strengths and weaknesses of the first few lines of the dogs in their pedigrees, where specific traits come from, both desirable and unwanted. The successful breeder wishing to ensure high quality puppies will also do their homework and look for a prepotent sire, who has a good track record of producing outstanding progeny to a range of bitches, imposing their own characteristics over the recessive genes of their dams. Or conversely, those with strong dams may look for a stud dog that appears to add nothing much to the mix, if they want the qualities of their excellent bitches to shine through.

HEALTH

In addition to producing a 'type', good breeders will have a very strong handle on health issues affecting their breed. This is an extremely important part of the mix, because without a sound dog all your hard work (in training) will amount to nothing – to say nothing of the heartache that a crippling or life-threatening condition can cause.

I would not consider purchasing a puppy from a breeder who had not ensured that all the baseline health tests recommended for the breed had been conducted for both sire and dam, as well as *myKC online portal provides health information on UK Kennel Club-registered dogs for breeders and puppy buyers to use. (Photo: UK Kennel Club, September 2019)*

understanding the DNA status for some of the recessive conditions that can be passed on. For example, for Labradors this would mean hip and elbow X-rays and scores for both sire and dam, as well as current clear eye tests. In addition, one of the parents should have been tested clear for hereditary conditions such as progressive retinal atrophy (PRA), centronuclear myopathy (CNM), exercise-induced collapse (EIC) and skeletal dysplasia/dwarfism (SD2), to ensure that their progeny is born unaffected by these diseases.

The myKC online service is an excellent resource provided by the UK Kennel Club, and is free to use once you have registered. It provides health-related information on all dogs registered with the Kennel Club. You can use it to find all the relevant information for the sire and dam of your proposed litter, so you can check that all health tests have been carried out, and see the results.

Within this vast database is the 'estimated breeding value' (EBV) tool, which evaluates the genetic value of an individual dog in relation to the whole of that dog's breed for hip and elbow

dysplasia – arguably the two most structurally debilitating diseases that are known to affect Labradors, Golden Retrievers, Irish Water Spaniels and to a lesser extent Flat Coated Retrievers.

EBVs are intended to help breeders mitigate against the risk of these disorders, by providing statistical information. They are created using the hip and elbow scores not only for the dog in question but for all of its relatives (including sire, dam, siblings, progeny and so on). So it gives a much fuller picture than just looking at an individual dog's score.

For example, an EBV of zero is the 'centre line' and reflects the average over the last ten years of the breed. Readings into the green (with a minus score) show an animal to have a better than average chance of producing good scoring offspring. Whereas a score into the red (and confusingly with a positive score) would be an animal that is more of a risk at producing offspring with worse than average hip and/or elbow scores.

The EBV data is only updated quarterly, so it does take a while for recent data to filter through

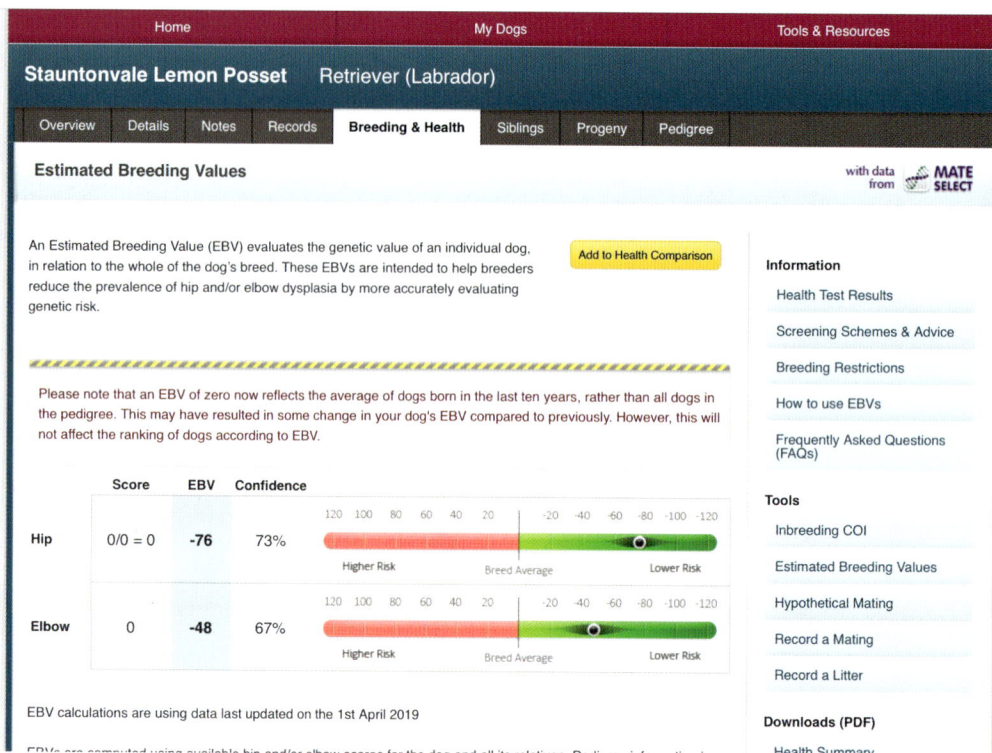

Estimated Breeding Values

with data from **MATE SELECT**

An Estimated Breeding Value (EBV) evaluates the genetic value of an individual dog, in relation to the whole of the dog's breed. These EBVs are intended to help breeders reduce the prevalence of hip and/or elbow dysplasia by more accurately evaluating genetic risk.

Add to Health Comparison

Information

Health Test Results

Screening Schemes & Advice

Breeding Restrictions

How to use EBVs

Frequently Asked Questions (FAQs)

Please note that an EBV of zero now reflects the average of dogs born in the last ten years, rather than all dogs in the pedigree. This may have resulted in some change in your dog's EBV compared to previously. However, this will not affect the ranking of dogs according to EBV.

Tools

Inbreeding COI

Estimated Breeding Values

Hypothetical Mating

Record a Mating

Record a Litter

	Score	EBV	Confidence			
Hip	0/0 = 0	-76	73%	120 100 80 60 40 20 │ -20 -40 -60 -80 -100 -120	Higher Risk	Breed Average	Lower Risk
Elbow	0	-48	67%	120 100 80 60 40 20 │ -20 -40 -60 -80 -100 -120	Higher Risk	Breed Average	Lower Risk

EBV calculations are using data last updated on the 1st April 2019

Downloads (PDF)

Health Summary

Ideally breeders should be working to reduce the risk of potential joint issues by selecting a sire and dam that have better than average EBV scores – 'in the green band' – with a high degree of confidence. (Photo: UK Kennel Club, September 2019)

and inform breedings. The tool evaluates genetic risk, not taking into account environmental effects. Using EBVs to make mating decisions is more comprehensive than merely looking at individual scores for hips and elbows alone, and as more data is added, it will enable breeders to progress in reducing the prevalence of these two diseases.

With the use of the degree of Confidence reading, expressed as a percentage, we begin to get a better understanding of those individuals at higher risk of passing on a condition to their offspring, and those that are a lower risk. This Confidence reading is a measure of how much information has been used to calculate the EBV. If the dog has been scored itself as well as having several relatives with scores, and progeny, then the degree of Confidence will be higher, as the information is more accurate. The more information that is available, then the more accurate the EBV will be.

As a result, the EBV for any dog will change throughout its lifetime. At birth a puppy will start with an EBV that is the average of its two parents. But once this pup is scored, and more data is used to populate the picture of its siblings, aunts, uncles and so on, then this score will move either up or down.

Like any system, it isn't foolproof, and relies on the data that is entered. Therefore, if scores from dogs are omitted because they were too bad, or if owners do not get their pups scored, then the picture will obviously be incomplete or skewed. But overall, it gives breeders (and puppy buyers) a really good resource to use when researching potential matings.

TEMPERAMENT

In any consideration of breeding, temperament is another extremely important factor, and is possibly a term that is used a lot, but not thoroughly understood. The dictionary definition is 'a person's or animal's nature, especially as it permanently affects their behaviour'. Largely, we want our retrievers to be sociable, friendly, benign and biddable, but with ample helpings

Retrievers will spend far more of their time not actually working, but waiting patiently and calmly, either on a drive at a shoot or in the gallery at a trial. They need to have the right temperament to be able to 'switch off'.

of bravery, commitment, drive, style and passion. In short, we want a thoroughly rounded, bomb-proof working dog that is also at ease in the gun bus or in the pub!

In addition to this comprehensive wish list, I would lay another requirement on to my ideal dog, which I call 'temperament to trial'. This is a dog's ability to be driven and committed in its work, with the desire to get the job done, but also for it to be calm and composed at heel or on the peg. This is not a given by any means. Some people are wary of buying a puppy with 'too much red' in its pedigree as they feel it will be a fire-breather and too hot to handle, and this can sometimes be true, without knowledge of the dogs in question, and the ability to focus and channel their drive.

Any good shooting dog needs to have an 'off' switch as well as an 'on' switch. And a dog will quickly learn the routines of waiting patiently during a drive, and then being asked to retrieve at the end. However, a dog used for trialling will also have a new set of 'routines' in that it may be taken to a two-day trial and walked in the gallery for hours on end before its turn. There, it needs to remain relaxed and calm with the twenty-plus other dogs and their handlers, before it goes into line, possibly walking up for another hour or so. Once in line, it needs to switch on and be alert for every bird shot, which could potentially be

its next retrieve (or not). A day or two later, the same dog may be out picking up again in heavy drives. Our working gundogs are truly versatile and must have the temperament to suit their jobs.

When you are evaluating temperament, there are no established tests. It is something that you have to do through research. And sometimes it is difficult to work out, when regarding behaviour, what is 'nature' and what is 'nurture', because much social behaviour is environmentally created or trained.

MORE THAN HALF THE STORY?

As I have mentioned, our own kennel is a little different because we have built it up on bitches, whereas the majority of competitive trialling people run male dogs, which is more practical because they don't come into season. However, I place huge importance on the quality of a bitch line in breeding, and our kennel has been established through this strength. To date it includes five champion bitches.

You will often hear people debating the input of the dam, and some believe that it contributes more than 50 per cent of the mix to puppies. There is one study on thoroughbred racehorses (Lin *et al*, 2015) whereby the findings do suggest that the maternal line makes a statistically significant difference when breeding for athletic performance.

In any mating, the sire and dam each contribute exactly half the alleles on the autosomal chromosomes, which include all the chromosomes except the X and Y sex chromosomes. However, the mitochondria are solely inherited from the mother. They are found in every cell of the body, and it is their job to produce ATP (adenosine triphosphate), a high energy molecule, which is the chemical 'fuel' of the body.

Lin's study speculates that the variation in the maternally inherited mitochondria could contribute towards differences in performance in the offspring. The hypothesis is that dams with more powerful mitochondria pass the trait to their progeny. This may be a benefit in racehorses, but it would only relate to one aspect of a sporting dog. And there seem to be no comparable studies in dogs that support the notion that the dam is of greater importance genetically in determining the quality of puppies produced.

In relation to the X and Y sex chromosomes, a male pup will inherit the Y chromosome from his father (XY) and the X chromosome from his mother (XX). And a female pup will inherit the X chromosome from both her father and mother. Logically then, the female pup will have 50 per cent X-relatedness to her paternal grandmother, whereas the male pup will have 0 per cent X-relatedness to the paternal grandmother. And both will have 25 per cent X-relatedness to the maternal grandmother.

Most genes, however, are not on the sex chromosomes – the X chromosome only accounts for around 8 per cent of the genes in humans – but it is an interesting consideration when analysing pedigrees and the input from grandparents. I had always had a hunch about the importance of grandparents in pedigrees, and felt pups were 'throwing' towards their grandmothers (my own paternal grandmother had a very big impact on my life, in some of our shared passions and interests). This mode of inheritance in the sex chromosomes seems to support that feeling.

ALTERING GENE EXPRESSION

Having briefly touched on the role of 'nurture' above in relation to temperament and behaviour, let's look at this whilst evaluating the importance of the dam. The following factors are bound to have an effect on puppies: maternal environment, the dam's nutrition and her interactions with the pups. In this respect, the quality of the dam and her home environment has more of an influence on the quality of the resulting offspring than any sire can have.

In addition, we can consider the role of epigenetics – how organisms change by modification of gene expression, rather than alteration of the genetic code itself. That is, it is not just genes that make our pups, but inheritance being influenced by mechanisms other than through the DNA sequence of genes. For example, researchers found that chronic exposure to stress hormones caused changes to DNA in the brains of mice, in turn prompting changes in gene expression (Lee

et al, 2010). In this way, the dam and her environment may have a more significant role to play in the way cells in the puppies read genes, turning on either positive or negative effects.

WHO'S THE DADDY?

If the bitch line is so important, or at least as important, why then do people always ask who the sire is?! Probably because they are the ones that we have usually heard of, because they are Field Trial Champions or popular sires of the day. There are still only a handful of Field Trial Champion Labrador bitches, compared to dogs. Of the twenty Labrador Field Trial Champions that gained their title during the 2017/18 season, sixteen were dogs and just four were bitches (data UK Kennel Club). No Golden Retrievers or Flat Coated Retrievers achieved their title in the same year.

Furthermore at the IGL Retriever Championship 2017, of the sixty qualifiers, forty were Labrador dogs and eighteen were Labrador bitches (with one Golden Retriever dog, and one Golden Retriever bitch). Of those qualified Labrador dogs, twenty-four were Field Trial Champions, and of the bitches, ten were Field Trial Champions.

Whereas a bitch can only have four litters registered with the UK Kennel Club (which would amount to around just twenty-five to thirty-five puppies), a well-used stud can be responsible for literally hundreds (and sometimes thousands) of puppies. So it is more likely that we will have heard of a certain sire because most Field Trial Champions are male, and a lot of breeders seek out these well-known dogs to use on their bitches.

With a bitch, you will always have to work around her seasons, and if you wish to take a litter from her too, this will take additional time out of her training year, whilst she is in whelp and then caring for her puppies. A dog, on the other hand, can potentially train and compete or work throughout the entire year.

CHOOSING A PUPPY

From all of the above, you will see that a great deal of careful thought and planning goes in to a well-bred litter by an experienced and respected breeder. Most owners and trainers don't want

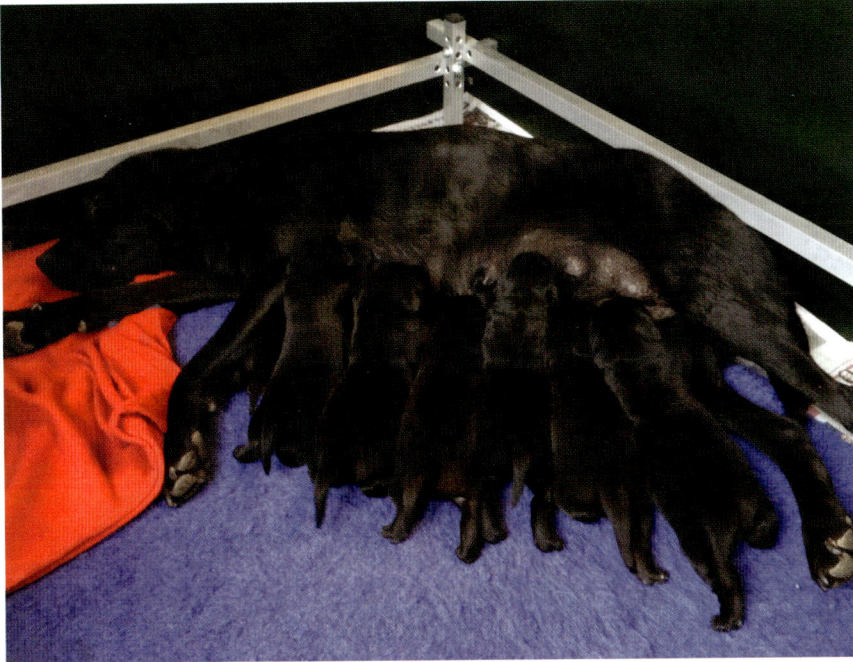

Some breeders venture to tell you 'that one is independent/bold/laid back', whilst others swear by puppy temperament testing to determine individual characteristics. But I genuinely believe there is no way of knowing the future potential of any individual puppy at such a tender age. Personality traits are by no means set in stone, and if we test a pup one day, it may well score differently another day, depending on factors including whether it is tired, has just eaten, or is playing with its siblings. My main requirement would be a bright, sociable pup that enjoys my company and gives me some eye contact.

to go down the breeding route themselves, and therefore have to rely on breeders to act responsibly and produce healthy, sound and fit-for-function puppies.

I often get asked 'how do you choose a puppy?' My answer is straightforward. I tell people to put a lot more time and effort into choosing a breeder or litter than selecting the actual puppy itself. Do your homework thoroughly (and the internet is a great asset here), researching not only the intended sire and dam and their work record and health tests, but also what that breeder has produced in the past, and the types of dog that he/she breeds and handles. Once you have found the litter that meets your requirements, I would simply go with your heart. Pick one that catches your eye. At eight weeks, the rest is down to pot luck.

Good breeders will have long waiting lists, so you may need to be prepared to put your name down and wait for the right litter. But this is a worthwhile wait, if you bear in mind that you will be spending more than a decade with your chosen pup.

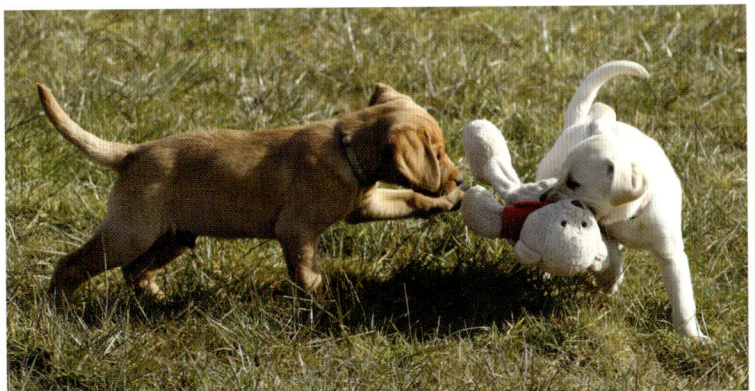

It is impossible to predict the potential of a puppy whilst it is still with its litter mates.

THE BEST STARTING POINT

Sound breeding makes life much easier for the trainer. Finding the type and temperament of dog that suits your training style and personality makes the world of difference. Certain lines have particular qualities, and in our own kennel we have tried to nurture what was good in the bitches we have and complement that with qualities from the sires we chose to use on them. When choosing a suitable sire for our litters, we look beyond the dog and its own individual characteristics, and more towards what it has produced to other similar bitches in the past. Sometimes what you see is not what you get. Using an older dog with progeny already out in the field gives you a lot more to go on, than taking a guess on a younger dog with unproven progeny.

Over the years we have gained a lot more knowledge about temperament and health, and now use tools such as the Kennel Club Estimated Breeding Values and Coefficient of Inbreeding when we select sires to improve the overall health of our line. Of course, it's not foolproof. But it mitigates risk to an extent. So much work goes into training a working retriever so the basis needs to be a healthy, sound dog.

TRAINING

> Success is no accident. It is hard work, perseverance, learning, studying, sacrifice, and most of all, love of what you are doing or learning to do.
> Pele, Brazilian footballer

My second fundamental building block, once I have got my breeding right, is training. And it is this that will form the focus of this book. But what exactly do we mean by 'training'? The *Cambridge Dictionary* definition is 'the process of learning the skills you need to do a particular job or activity'. This is fairly straightforward when you apply it to something such as learning how to play chess, knit or high jump, as we are only teaching ourselves.

However, with retriever training, there are two elements to the equation. We are looking not only at our dog's learning – his schooling to be a working retriever – but also at our own education – to become a proficient handler and trainer. Most gundog training instruction books focus on the first aspect – imparting the knowledge, routines and skill sets to our dogs. But I believe we are more than half the equation in this relationship, and so we should start our training journey by looking at ourselves. In Chapter 2, we will be doing this in some detail.

Retriever training is a partnership between handler and dog.

PUTTING IN THE HOURS

We've all heard the adage 'practice makes perfect', meaning the more we apply ourselves to a skill, the better we are likely to become. Effort applied definitely reaps rewards. Anders Ericsson, a Swedish psychologist, put forward the suggestion that 10,000 hours of focus and practice in your chosen field can make you an expert. Ericsson (2016) studied a group of violinists in Germany and focused on the factors that differentiated the best musicians from the mediocre ones. The group was asked to keep detailed records of how they spent their time, both on violin practice and daily activities. The research revealed that the top violinists spent considerably more time practising alone than the others did.

This finding was popularized by Malcolm Gladwell in his book *Outliers* (2009), where he stated: 'The thing that distinguishes one performer from another is how hard he or she works. That's it. And what's more, the people at the very top don't work just harder or even much harder than everyone else. They work much, *much* harder.'

The tenet appears to be that expertise is largely a matter of how much somebody practises, and this doesn't take into account any degree of 'talent' that might make it easier for someone to pick up the skills they require. This does seem to be a rather simplistic view, as there are undoubtedly people who have more aptitude for certain tasks or skills than others.

However, Ericsson says that his research was misinterpreted by Gladwell, and that just repeating the same activity over and over again is not sufficient to turn somebody into an expert. According to Ericsson, you need to engage in 'deliberate practice', whereby you don't just mindlessly repeat activities, but step outside your comfort zone and apply yourself in a focused way. Just repeating skills that you have already learnt is not enough to help you improve.

So, let us apply this principle to our lives training gundogs. If we dedicated fifteen hours a week to training working retrievers, this would mean that we might reasonably expect to become an expert in the field within thirteen years. For those people with full-time jobs, fifteen hours a week in the winter (when daylight hours are sparse) may seem unachievable. But 'deliberate practice' doesn't just mean doing the activity, but also time spent planning it and thinking about it in a critical way. All of which is valuable, focused activity.

And just for fun, if we went one step further and applied this same concept to our dogs, we

UK Field Trial Champion Labradors that gained their title in 2017/18 (breakdown by age)	
Age	Number of dogs
3 years	4
4 years	6
5 years	4
6 years	4
7 years	2
Total	20
Source: UK Kennel Club (2019)	

might expect them to become experts themselves (with only ten hours practice a week, because we can't rely on them doing the planning and critical thinking part!) in under three years – as a dog year is widely thought to be equivalent to seven human years. This does seem to fit in with our timeframe of training working retrievers, in that we might reasonably consider them to be fully trained, and at their prime, between three to five years of age.

In addition to dedicated practice, there are, of course, other factors to consider including temperament, cognitive ability, socio-economic factors, age, quality of tuition, physical ability, genes, environment and so on, many of which apply to both the trainer and the dog.

Recent research (Brooke Macnamara *et al*, 2016) has confirmed that while deliberate practice did account for some of the differences between athletes (some 18 per cent of variance in performance), it didn't account for all of them. These researchers also found that 'athletes who reached a high level of skill did not begin their sport earlier in childhood than lower skill athletes. This finding challenges the notion that higher skill performers tend to start in a sport at a younger age than lower skill performers.' Their conclusions, therefore, were that a wide range of factors has to be taken into consideration in understanding expertise.

WORK SMART, NOT HARD

People often say to me 'You must train all the time to have achieved what you have', or 'How often do you train?' Yes, I have definitely put in the work, but not in the way that many people might imagine. I don't spend every waking hour training. In fact, my friends know I am a bit of a 'fair weather' trainer! But I can justify this approach. I don't go out if I don't truly feel like it. My feeling is that no dog ever got ruined by spending a bit of extra time in the kennel or the kitchen for a day off, or going for a nice walk instead. But plenty have been set back in some way with a bad training session that lacked thought and planning, and ended in frustration.

I do, however, spend a lot of time thinking about the dogs and their training. With Pru (my first champion) I was extremely methodical with her education. I put in the time, in a structured format, and recorded it in a meticulous way. This enabled me to see that her training was comprehensive, leaving no base uncovered. Over the years I have become much more 'organic' in my approach, and perhaps more efficient. I use less formal structure, and adapt as I go along to the dog in front of me.

It's not about 'how much' but more about the quality – concentrating on this rather than quantity. Ten minutes spent on a focused activity or exercise is usually far more beneficial than going out for hours on end just to give the dog some retrieves or socialize with other handlers and dogs.

My late father used to say 'work smart, not hard', although I don't think it was necessarily a principle that he lived by himself. He definitely had a strong work ethic. But his words still play in my head, and sometimes, if the weather is particularly horrible, I can use them as a simple justification to not go out training. If it's not enjoyable for both you and the dog, then I do question 'why do it'?

You need to be in the right frame of mind to train. If you don't think you are going to get the best out of a dog, or yourself, by training that day, then don't go out. There is no point in just training for the sake of training. There has to be a benefit to the dog/handler partnership.

RAINY DAY TRAINING

The point about not going out in bad weather is an insouciant one, of course, as we do have to eventually accustom our dogs (and ourselves) to working in all weathers. But on days when you can't go out, or don't want to, for whatever reason, try to use that time to support your practical training. There is plenty you can do indoors, not least of which is studying and thinking. For example, I read books and magazines, or watch video clips, not just about gundogs but also in related areas, such as animal behaviour and learning theory. This enables me to broaden my own education and take a more strategic approach to training.

Reading around your subject will give you new ideas, techniques and philosophies that you can apply to your own dogs. It allows you to experiment with different methods to see what works best. It will also help you to deepen your understanding of your dogs and how they learn.

HOUSE STYLE

At Stauntonvale, our own training style is flexible, modern and reward based, and I will detail some of our techniques in Part Two of this book. We employ a thoughtful approach that entails being adaptive and considering the dog in front of you, analysing how each individual dog is learning, and changing methods to suit its needs. My background in communications, along with having a very analytical mind, has helped me with relating to both handlers and their dogs. In addition, being a breeder as well as a trainer has allowed my own 'house style' to develop over the years.

We are breeding intelligent, biddable and stylish dogs with the required amount of drive, and this makes my job as a trainer easier. It really does help to have the best 'starting material'.

FEEDING

> When you give your body the best possible fuel, you have more energy, you're stronger, you think more quickly.
>
> Michelle Obama, former First Lady

My final 'building block' is nutrition. And this is, perhaps, the topic that causes the most debate at training groups and in online forums and on social media. We all like to feel we are doing the best for our dogs with our feeding regime, and we all have an opinion on it. Some suggest that an all raw food diet is best, whereas others rely on a 'complete' formulated dry food for convenience. In multi-dog households, feeding decisions are often governed by economics, too.

My interest in canine nutrition started when I planned my first litter from Pru (Field Trial Champion Jobeshill Octavia) in 2010. I wanted to make sure both mother and the litter had the very best possible nutritional support. That meant finding the right food for them, and something that was convenient to use all the time. After extensive research, I came across a grain-free food from Canada, ORIJEN, which had only recently been introduced into the UK as one of the first grain-free commercial dog foods. The high meat content (80 per cent), coupled with the brand's biologically appropriate philosophy, caught my eye. From my research, I knew that a lot of dry dog food contains fillers that provide no nutritional value to dogs – so I wanted to make sure that my pups had the very best start. This food had exactly the right mix of high meat protein, moderate fat and low carbohydrate that I was looking for.

Dogs have been a companion to humans for thousands of years. However, despite the dog's long association with humans and its domestication, it evolved as a hunter and still shares 99 per cent of its DNA with the wolf. And although we like to humanize our faithful companion, a dog's nutritional needs are fundamentally different to our own, based on anatomy and physiology.

Dogs evolved as carnivores, not omnivores. Although the domestic dog has changed dramatically in physical appearance from its wild ancestors, the basic physiology of the modern dog has altered very little with domestication. Dogs are not only capable of eating the food of their wild ancestors, they actually require it for optimum health. Their short digestive tracts and gastrointestinal systems are adapted to metabolize animal flesh and fat, not grains and carbohydrates. In fact, as long as enough protein is given, the dog has no requirement for carbohydrates.

THE GIGO PRINCIPLE

Dogs are very adaptable, but just because they can survive on an omnivorous diet doesn't mean that this is the best diet for them. There's a big difference between 'survive' and 'thrive', and running competitive gundogs requires a little more than just the ability to exist! We ask a lot from our dogs, expecting them to perform in all weathers, working in often demanding conditions. For that, they need to be at their peak in physical and mental fitness. I've always believed in putting the best in to get the very best out, and that philosophy runs not only throughout our breeding and training programmes, but also in the way that we feed our dogs.

Modern 'complete' feeds are prolific now, and offer a convenient way to feed our dogs, especially if we are on the road. However, many dry dog food manufacturers focus on cost when formulating their feeds, at the expense of appropriate nutrition. Pet food makers are producing foods designed primarily for their appeal to consumers (after all, your dog never goes out shopping for itself). This means focusing on lowering costs and increasing convenience, rather than making a food that is most appropriate for the dog.

Grains and carbohydrates are used in dry feeds as an inexpensive source of calories. They are readily available and easy to process, transport and store. The majority of complete dry dog foods contain more than 50 per cent grain, and are high in carbohydrate and relatively low in protein. And even the so-called 'super premium' and 'holistic' dry dog foods still contain over 40 per cent grain and 40–50 per cent carbohydrate.

Protein is of crucial importance for dogs. It is essential for basic body functions, cellular regeneration, tissue maintenance, hormone and enzyme production, as well as the provision of energy. High quality animal proteins, considered 'complete proteins', contain all the amino acids essential to dogs, in quantities that match the requirements needed for their overall health, maintenance and growth.

Whilst plants also contain some proteins (for example, corn gluten), they don't contain all the amino acids in the right proportions to meet a dog's needs. Protein also needs to be in a digest-

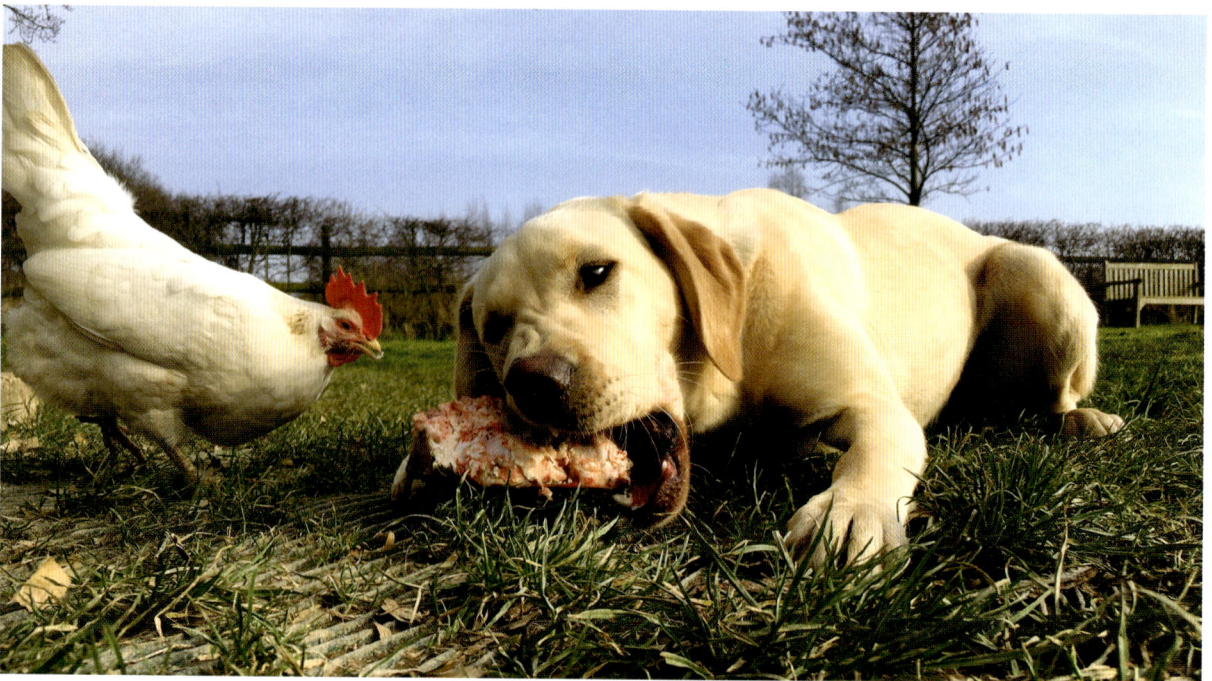

Raw meaty bones are an excellent way to keep your dog's teeth clean, removing plaque build-up.

Pups benefit from 'top up' feeds from mum as they grow bigger.

ible form for dogs, and their short digestive tract means that plant proteins are far less digestible than meat protein.

And then there's the testy question of fat. We live in a culture where we are conditioned to think that fat is bad, and that 'fat free' is good. But that simply doesn't apply to dogs. Unlike us, dogs don't suffer from cholesterol problems caused by high levels of animal fats. Fat is an extremely important part of dog nutrition, providing a concentrated supply of energy and essential fatty acids (EFAs) not otherwise synthesized in the body. Dogs metabolize fat just as we metabolize carbohydrates. Fat is their fuel, providing them with the ability to function at their peak. Dogs require a fairly high amount of fat in their diets, and this, again, should be sourced from animals not plants.

So, what is the appropriate diet for a dog? A biologically appropriate diet mirrors the same balance and variety of ingredients that would be eaten in the wild (including meat, bone, fat, organs and vegetables). Biologically appropriate foods are designed to match the digestive capability of dogs. This is straightforward if you are feeding raw. Applied to dry foods, the concept means higher protein, moderate fat, low carbo-hydrate foods that contain a high proportion of animal ingredients that are processed as little as possible.

FUELLING THE ATHLETE

We all know somebody who can regale us with tales of such-and-such a dog that lived to a grand old age and was fed just table scraps and porridge. Or another that was fed the cheapest dry food but always 'did well'. And the same goes for humans, too. But when we look at sporting endeavour at the higher levels, 'food is fuel' but it is also a whole lot more than that.

Speak to the professional athlete and they will extol the virtues of how correct nutrition helps give them that extra edge. Diets are micromanaged, with different foods eaten at various times of the day, ensuring optimum performance whether the athlete is in training or competition. The same principle applies to our canine athletes. Whether it is greyhound racing, agility or gundog field trials, consistently producing 'champions' requires ensuring they have the right food to complement their training and performance. Fats and lipids are a great source of energy, so maintaining a high fat level in our sporting dogs' diet is crucial. Likewise, protein is the essential building block for tissue and muscle repair.

Whilst nutrition is important for all animals, for sporting dogs it is critical that they are fed the right foods from an early age, to develop the necessary muscle to support their joints and build a solid foundation for their future development and growth. Scientists (such as Riser 1975) have pointed out that biomechanical diseases, such as hip dysplasia, come about when there is a disparity between primary muscle mass and rapid skeletal growth – that is, when muscles fail to develop and reach functional maturity at the same time as the skeleton. So, whilst there is undoubtedly a hereditary element to these conditions, nutrition also undoubtedly has a role to play.

FUNCTIONAL FOODS

And it's not just about performance, but overall health too. We should look at nutrition at a cellular level, and the role it plays in cell maintenance and inflammation. Food can send signals to the epigenome (the chemical compounds that tell the genome what to do). In turn, these compounds attach to DNA, marking the genome and changing the way the cells use the DNA's instruc-

tions – turning genes on or off.

It is really important to feed a diet rich in 'functional foods' (nutritional ingredients such as amino acids, vitamins and certain botanicals) that signal the epigenome for healthy gene expression, and to reduce or eliminate foods that send harmful messages to the epigenome, triggering unhealthy gene expression/cell inflammation. In a nutshell, food plays a role in cell inflammation, signalling either good or bad things to happen to cells. In this way, nutrition can be used to control conditions such as arthritis, cancer, heart disease and other common canine health issues.

Functional nutrition is a complex subject in its own right, and one that is beyond the scope of this book. For those who are interested in reading more about the topic, I would recommend Jean Dodds' book *Canine Nutrigenomics* (2015). It provides a valuable insight into the role that various foods play, and can be related not only to our dogs' diets but also to our own.

FEEDING STRATEGIES

At Stauntonvale we feed our dogs twice a day, to spread the load, so that each meal is smaller

Pups enjoying early independent feeds as part of the weaning process.

and more digestible. Also, it is advisable to give the larger amount of food post- rather than pre-exercise. Some people actually advise fasting prior to performance, but we maintain a regular meal schedule whether it is a rest day, a training day or a competition day – although we always ensure any training or work is done at least an hour after a meal to avoid the risk of torsion. And if the dog is undergoing a lot of sustained work throughout the day, we will supplement with a lunchtime snack (something high fat/high protein) to 'top up' the dog before the evening meal.

With young pups, divide their food over three or four meals a day, and maintain this regime throughout their greatest growth period, up to around six to seven months. Pups need a large volume of food compared to adult dogs, but if this is given in fewer meals it can lead to them just eliminating the excess (in the form of loose stools), and consequently not gaining the benefit from it. Spreading the same amount of food over a greater number of feeds can also help when trying to add, or maintain, weight on a skinny dog.

In addition to food, consider the dog's fluid intake. When the dog is working hard, he will obviously pant more, as well as sweating from his feet. Lack of fluids will result in loss of concentration and poor work. It is therefore vital to keep the canine athlete well hydrated. Even throughout winter, consider carrying water and a bowl with you, to ensure your dog has the necessary hydration.

2 THE OTHER END OF THE LEAD

Fairly early on in my gundog journey I read Lance Armstrong's book *It's Not About the Bike* (2001), whose title now feels somewhat ironic, and it hit a chord with me. It was just after I had been struggling with the wilful Nellie, so in my mind I was feeling 'it's all about the dog'. But what it did do was inspire me, and make me realize the importance of myself in the equation. It isn't just about the dog, or the training equipment, or resources. It is all about me and my attitude. The human factor is really important, and something we need to get right before we can begin to train the dog effectively.

So in this chapter we explore what is going on at the 'other end of the lead'. It may seem strange to start a gundog training book by looking at yourself. But if you are not in the right place, then how can you expect to help and guide your dog through its education? This is a partnership, after all.

BELIEVE IN YOURSELF

One of the commonest things that I see with handlers when they come to me for guidance is their lack of confidence when handling their dog. This is usually apparent through their body language, for example in the way they walk with their dog at heel. They are tentative and show concern, worried to put a foot out of place, or they change their pace to suit that of the dog. Others, when giving commands, sound very uncertain themselves. If I am noticing this, then you can be sure that the dog is, too. Dogs are masters of body language, as it is their main form of communication. They are constantly watching us and trying to 'read' us.

Confidence when handling and training a dog is critical. You need to maintain control of your own emotions. If you are feeling nervous or lacking in confidence, then how can you expect your dog to take direction from you? Your feelings will quickly transfer to the dog. Learn to pay attention to your body language and posture, as well as your tone of voice and whistle.

Body language do's and don'ts	
Do...	*Don't...*
Stand up straight with shoulders back	Slump
Walk positively, at *your* speed	Use a tense posture or hold your breath
Use 'open'/welcoming body language	'Crowd' your dog on sendaway, or lunge towards your dog on delivery
Use eye contact	Wear sunglasses

Many of the people whom I train are extremely successful in their business and personal lives. They are capable, strong individuals, in control of their own destinies. But often that capability seems to go to pieces when they start handling a dog, and they end up ceding control of the situation, or watching helplessly as things start to go wrong. I see handlers walking on eggshells beside their dog, slumping in resignation if handling is prolonged, or pleading through a stop whistle.

With novice handlers, it is natural to lack confidence and belief in your own abilities, as you are still learning your trade. But when you are directing a dog you need to act in control, even

SELF CONFIDENCE AND SELF-BELIEF

I've recommended a great little book to some of my friends and students – *Self-Confidence: the remarkable truth of why a small change can make a big difference* by Paul McGee (2010).

The following are the main takeaway points, which relate to your role as a retriever trainer:

Accept your flaws: They make us what we are. Nobody is perfect, and that's okay. Be aware of your weaknesses, but don't see them as 'faults'. You can still be flawed and fabulous. This applies to dogs, too!

Quit beating yourself up: Stop fretting about the mistakes you have made. Focus instead on making small steps forwards. Don't dwell on mistakes, but use them to learn by. It's hard not to take problems as set-backs, but try to bounce back and be creative to find a constructive way forwards. Sometimes only by going wrong can you learn how to go right.

Get a grip and take control: Start driving. Be in charge of your journey. Steer towards where you want to go. Who drove the car to the lesson? Don't hand the car keys over to the dog once you get to the training field.

Don't wait for confidence – it could be a long wait: Hiding behind the novice label will only hold you back. It is possible to go out there and 'get it'. Make a decision and go for it. I ran in my first field trial in September 2005 – four years later I was running in the IGL Retriever Championship (with a different dog) and made her up into a champion that same year.

Weigh up criticism: Evaluate the feedback that you get. Don't evade it. Seek it out, but don't let it erode your confidence. Learn from it. You may gain valuable insights that will help you to achieve your goals.

if you are feeling far from it! You can't expect a dog to believe in you if you don't look or sound as if you really know what you are doing yourself.

For many, then, improving your training and handling will actually start with increasing your own self-confidence and self-belief.

GETTING THE RIGHT HELP

To enjoy success on your gundog journey, you need to have a strategy for your training. Whilst much early foundation work can be done on your own using books and DVDs for guidance, there will come a time when you are ready to take your young dog out in company, to attend a lesson. This may be with a local gundog club. Or you might decide to seek out the expertise of a professional gundog trainer. Help from others with more experience is invaluable in making progress.

Find a good trainer who trains and handles a dog in a style that you admire, and seek a private lesson with them. Being able to train and handle a dog yourself is one thing – being able to impart that knowledge and teach others is something else. So it is best to ask around for a recommendation as to a trainer who could become a suitable mentor. Not only does your trainer need to be a great dog-person and handler themselves, but they must also be able to communicate effectively to help you achieve your own training goals. They need to be able to analyse what you and your dog are doing, and to give you a clear strategy on how to make changes for improvement.

Try to keep with just one trainer initially, while you are in a 'novice' phase of training. Each trainer will have their own individual style and methods, and these may differ widely. Staying with one trainer will give you some consistency

A good trainer will become a mentor to you, and will be able to explain the advice they give, and why it is appropriate for your dog. (Photo: John Jeffrey)

to your training, and that trainer will work with you to find what best meets the needs of your individual dog.

Trying to take on advice from too many different sources at an early stage can be overwhelming. And it becomes very difficult to 'sort the wheat from the chaff'. Several different opinions on a particular issue may be equally valid, and all may work with different dogs. There is usually more than one way to approach something, and quite often there is no 'right' or 'wrong' way. So trainer A might suggest solution X to your problem, and trainer B might suggest solution Y. But unfortunately, gundog training is not an exact science – it's more of an art, and this can become very confusing in your early days of training, when you don't have the confidence to know which solution will apply best to your own dog.

When a trainer tells you to do something a particular way, don't adopt that advice if you don't understand why it applies. And don't be afraid to ask why that particular method is appropriate, or how it will work. If the trainer can't explain why, then think twice before adopting that advice. Don't just take what a trainer says as gospel because you think they have a high status, or

because something was 'always done that way'. It doesn't mean that it will be right for your own dog.

Your trainer should be able to explain to you not only what to do, but why you should do it in that way. If this makes sense to you, then adopt it and give it a fair try. Don't be too hasty to dismiss it if it doesn't appear to be working straightaway. People sometimes attempt to do what their trainer has told them, but if it doesn't work after one or two attempts, they give up. Or they move on and try something else, or someone else. However, this isn't fair either to the trainer or to the dog. You need to apply what the trainer has suggested consistently and over a prolonged period of time, before reassessing how the solution is working.

A good teacher will give you feedback on your efforts, and will help you plan to achieve your goals, with realistic homework to do on your own. Eventually you will be able to spot problems yourself and adapt your training accordingly.

There will, of course, come a time in your training when you will want to take on the ideas of other trainers, and also get your dog out to different grounds and situations. This is important

Group training is ideal for preparing your dog to work in the company of other dogs and also to honour their work quietly and calmly.

not only to prove your training in a variety of terrains, but it will also help you avoid stagnation. A fresh pair of eyes can often give inspiration, or just an insight that will kick start your training again. Once you are experienced and more confident in your abilities as a trainer, it can be invaluable to be given new ideas or some additional input.

THE GROUP SITUATION

It is worth talking about group training here. Whilst your basic 'set-up' work can be done largely on your own, one of the few things you can't do on your own is train in a group. And proving your dog amongst other dogs and handlers is a critical part of its overall education. Around 80–90 per cent of a working retriever's day is spent doing 'nothing'. If he is sitting on a peg whilst you shoot, out picking up for the day, or waiting in line in a trial, he is required to con-

duct himself calmly and quietly, sitting, observing, but not actually retrieving. He needs to be able to watch other dogs work and maintain his composure.

Practising this aspect is extremely important. When you attend a group class, it really isn't all about the retrieves you get. Try and use your group time wisely in this respect, and when other dogs are working, rather than watching them, pay attention to how your dog is relating to those dogs and being in a group situation. Working in a group will give you the opportunity of honouring other dogs' work, and will also teach your dog skills such as running up the line of people and dogs, which can be intimidating at first, and maintaining good heelwork whilst walking up with others.

An important consideration with group training, though, is how *we* behave when we are in company – which is often very different to how we would act and react when we are training alone. Handlers understandably get more nervous when in a group, as they feel they are 'performing' in front of others, and are perhaps also being judged by them. There can also be a feeling of not wanting to take up too much of the limited group time when things go wrong. So handlers will accept things they might not otherwise be happy with when alone. Or they rush to pick the retrieve any way they can, without really thinking about what the dog is learning from the exercise. There is often an element of 'saving face' going on. It is important, then, to train in a group where you feel comfortable, either with friends or like-minded people who use similar styles and methods.

Sometimes handlers will excuse their dogs in company and say it's their own fault, taking the blame away from the dog, as nobody likes to feel their own dog is anything less than perfect. And sometimes (actually quite often) it *is* the handler's 'fault', although probably not in the way they are meaning. Usually problems occur because the dog is not adequately equipped for the scenario. This is just lack of background training and preparation.

Try to be a little selfish when you are in your group, not to the point where you are taking all the instructor's time and attention, but in respect of thinking 'what do I want to get out of this for my own dog?' – and remembering that you have paid to go there to improve your training and benefit the dog.

Sometimes a handler will say to me before a lesson, 'Oh, I hope Fido goes well today'. And often I will reply 'Well, I hope he doesn't!' I'm not being unkind. But my point is that training is where we should hope that our dogs *do* make mistakes, or show their weaknesses, as it is where we can address these issues and find strategies to overcome them. It's not a place to show off how brilliant your dog is – you can do that at a field trial, working test or on a shoot. Trainers are there to help you to find appropriate solutions and give you homework to help you improve.

I'm grateful when my own dogs don't go well in a training session, as it highlights areas for me to work on again when I'm on my own. By working on the highlighted issues, I can raise my game

for the actual performance in competition or in the shooting field. We become more polished. 'Poor' training days help me put things right for the future. Maybe there is some science after all in the saying that 'a bad dress rehearsal means a great opening night'?

BE AN INSPIRING LEADER

Having an experienced mentor can be invaluable, as they will get to know you and your dog, and will be able to give you help and input along your training journey. And as this person acts as a coach to you, so should you, too, think in these terms about your relationship with your dog.

The bond you build is extremely important, as you will hopefully be enjoying many years of sport together. So, rather than it being a 'master-servant' scenario, with the dog working for you, think of it in terms of 'coach-athlete'. It is up to you, as a coach, to bring out the best in your dog, and work together.

Ultimately you are looking to become a key part of a high functioning team – an inspirational leader. Your attitude, passion and commitment will be critical factors in your success. Great leaders have vision, are determined and inspiring, authentic in their actions, and with clear intentions. They act decisively, understanding their own identity but with the ability to show empathy. They are also aware of their own limitations and weaknesses.

Good leaders are able to maintain control of their emotions and act in a calmly assertive manner. These are important qualities for any dog trainer. As Patricia McConnell (2007) in *For the Love of a Dog* says: 'Dogs seem to love people who are quiet, cool and collected, and who prefer sitting beside them over sitting beside others'.

ARISTOTLE: 'WE ARE WHAT WE REPEATEDLY DO'

Training is a habit. As we discussed earlier, *deliberate practice* makes perfect. But you need to practise the right behaviours and not allow any undesirable habits to become ingrained, and understand that for long-term success there

Act calmly but assertively to be a good leader and coach for your dog.

Advances in Research on Sport Exercise (2003), Eriksson noted that élite skaters spent more time than average skaters practising elements in their routines they hadn't yet mastered. In contrast, the average skaters were spending more time going over routines that they could already perform.

I have noticed a similar phenomenon with retriever handlers. One particular handler used to visit sporadically for lessons, but stopped attending after a while as her dog never performed very well on my ground. But she assured me it always went really well at another trainer's ground. I don't think there was anything particularly special about either location geographically. But what I do suspect was happening, was that the dog was being given familiar exercises on known ground and had mastered them. That is, it was being given things it could already do and was looking smart doing them. When it came to me, I was stretching her and the dog out of their comfort zone and the cracks were beginning to appear. Consequently, she opted to keep going back to the other trainer. It's easy, and gratifying, to practise the things we can already do. But it won't necessarily enable us to move further forwards.

may be sacrifices in short-term pleasure. Training should be fun, but you will sometimes go through periods that are more *endurable* than enjoyable.

You will need to move out of your comfort zone, beyond 'muscle memory', and extend your current abilities, pushing yourself and stretching your dog so that you both advance. Rather than engaging in mechanical repetition of known scenarios, just 'giving the dog a few retrieves', you should think instead about the aims of exercises and what might be a realistic progression.

In his book *Expert Performance in Sports:*

Repetitive training activities can feel satisfying but they are largely ineffective when it comes to

Keeping quiet, cutting out non-essential verbal communication, and maintaining a positive relaxed stance are all part of being a more effective, easy-to-understand handler.

gaining any improvement. To paraphrase a quote attributed to Henry Ford: 'If you always do what you've always done, you'll always get where you've always gone.' We do all need to practise success and reinforce behaviours to ensure they are fully engrained. But once they are, we also need to push out of our comfort zones and press on. That way real progress is made. Sometimes activities may not come easily or naturally, but real training involves being prepared to fail a bit until you eventually piece it all together to reach your goal. Don't be scared when things go wrong. Keep trying. Sometimes we need to go wrong in order to go right.

Handlers will often give something a go but are too ready to give up or change position (usually moving themselves much nearer to the dog,

or re-throwing a dummy) to simplify the exercise if the dog goes wrong. With a very young dog this might be appropriate, but it isn't always the best approach with dogs that are further on in their training. Depending on the nature of the dog (and this is something that we will look at in the next chapter) and the stage of training, I would suggest 'keeping at it' so that the dog can take away some learning from the exercise, even though the process itself might not be perfect and how you would eventually want it.

APPROPRIATE COMMUNICATION

To be an effective coach to our dog, we need to speak in a language that they understand. As members of two very different species, a lot of our communications are alien to each other. Humans, as primates, enjoy chattering away in vocal language and show affection with gestures such as hugs. Canines, on the other hand, have relatively few vocalizations and most of their communication is done through body posturing and eye, ear, mouth and tail set. We are grabbers and 'doers', whereas dogs are observers. Consequently, a lot of what we regard as 'normal' communication is lost in translation to our dogs.

It is up to us to change the way we communicate so that we 'speak' a language that our dogs understand. We need to tailor our style and be perceptive to their responses. Try to notice when your dog is feeling concerned, excited, overaroused or confused, and be proactive in how you deal with it.

Dogs don't understand the meaning of words, the actual semantics, but rather they just make associations with our vocal utterances. So we need to be thoughtful about how they form those links. Tone of voice is often more important to them than the particular words we say. For example, 'Fido, come here' said in a light tone with a smile on your face, is going to mean something very different to 'Fido, come here' said in a growling, cross and menacing tone with a frowning face. Each command will provoke a different reaction and behaviour within the dog. In the first instance, Fido may race back joyously to his handler anticipating that something nice is

Be ready to deliver appropriate, well-timed praise for behaviour that you want to endorse.

you do together can be done quietly or silently, other than when you give praise as feedback that he is doing what you want in relation to your commands. Try to keep in mind the following in your attitude to him: quiet, calm and consistent. This will remind you to make your communications appropriate at all times.

Often when things go wrong in training our natural instinct is to become louder and louder, whether that is shouting commands at a dog in the hope that he will respond to a louder, repeated command, or blowing our whistle harder. But think about this in relation to what we have taught the dog. A succinct stop whistle blown at normal, calm pressure is understood as a known and positive command to the dog. But when you blow twice as hard and four times as long, that isn't the same command at all. Don't be surprised if the dog doesn't interpret it as you would expect. Furthermore, blowing harder, because the dog doesn't seem to be responding, isn't going to make the command any more effective. It is unlikely that the dog has failed to hear. Dogs have a very acute sense of hearing, probably better than our own. It isn't a communications failure in this instance, but a case that the command has not been sufficiently

about to happen, whereas in the second instance he may well stay put, hesitate, or slink back, with his ears set back, concerned that all is not well in human-world. Think about your own body language, tones and posture when you communicate with your dog.

Cut out the chatter! We have already established that dogs aren't vocal animals, so our own commentary is mostly 'background noise' to them. Although it may feel rewarding and pleasant to hold a special conversation with your dog, in practical terms it has no value to him. And constant utterings can actually impede training progress as the dog tries to untangle the important words from the unnecessary ones. Try to leave out non-essential human language when you take your dog out training. Most of what trained and then generalized to the specific situation.

Finally, pay attention to the timing of your communications, not only in your commands but also with your feedback to the dog on his actions. This latter point is particularly important, and is something that we will be looking at in more depth in later chapters. When you offer a dog praise, you have to be absolutely sure that the dog is relating to exactly what you are praising, otherwise you may end up inadvertently endorsing an activity that you actually don't want. For example, shouting 'good lad' just after the dog has picked up a dummy (because you are delighted that he has eventually found it), but just after he has begun hunting on with it in his mouth, rather than returning directly to you, may sow the seed in the dog's mind that it is acceptable, and desirable, that he sniffs the ground or 'hunts on' after picking. The timing of that praise was inappropriate. The handler thinks he has praised the dog for picking, and the dog thinks he was praised for what he was doing at that point

instead. Far better to wait until the dog has fully committed to powering back to the handler and then praise at that point so that you are endorsing the behaviour that you actually do want. We will address this form of 'feedback training' in Chapter 4.

All the elements that we have looked at in this chapter relate to yourself as your dog's trainer, mentor and handler. By applying thought and intelligence you can increase your own effectiveness in coaching your dog. Time spent thinking about the training process is just as valuable, if not more so, than going out and putting in the miles in the field. With the rise of social media, it is very easy to get sucked into thinking that everyone is out there, at all the different training events and grounds that are increasingly becoming available, and that you are being left behind if you are 'just' staying at home. But your home work should not equate to nothing. Putting in the thought and time at home, on a one-to-one basis with your dog, will always be the most important part of your training. It forms the bedrock.

COMMUNICATION CHECKLIST

- **Pay attention to tone, not just content**
- **Cut out chatter**
- **Be aware of your body language**
- **Keep all commands consistent**
- **Be critical on timing**
- **Give appropriate feedback**

3 A DOG'S POINT OF VIEW

Dogs are very different from a lot of other animals we work with because they are hypersocial and hypersensitive to everything we do.

Temple Grandin (2009)

Humans are used to not only thinking in abstracts, but also to seeing the world in this way. We find ideas easy and are able to generalize concepts. Animals, on the other hand, don't see the world like this. They see actual things, and will notice the detail. Temple Grandin, associate professor at Colarado State University, drew comparisons between how animals and autistic people see things, and how animals are, in this way, much more detail oriented. They see things in terms of black and white, rather than shades of grey. She used her own autistic condition to help inform her work on animals and their view of the world around them. Much of her early work was based around the movement of farm animals, and improving their experience in humane slaughter systems, where she noticed something as seemingly insignificant as the way light hit a shiny surface, which would be enough to cause stress and panic for cows because they noticed this small detail. Grandin also looked at dogs, cats, horses and zoo animals, and how, by using knowledge of the way they perceived the world, they could be trained in an appropriate manner for their species.

In her book *Making Animals Happy* (2009), she turned her attention to looking at 'seeking', one of the core emotions detailed by neuroscientist Dr Jaak Panksepp (2005), and how it can be used in training dogs. Seeking is a pleasurable emotion that gives the animal the energy to go after its goal, whether that is sex, play, knowledge or warmth. It is the 'Christmas emotion' of looking forward to something, which is often more pleasurable in itself than the actual final *having*. Training dogs to retrieve is a perfect way to turn on their seeking emotion to stimulate pleasure. Gundog work, in this way, is intrinsically satisfying for dogs. Chasing after a thrown dummy or running to a rabbit that has been shot is highly rewarding in itself, as it employs the seeking emotion. But this activity has to be carried out within parameters set by us as handlers. The traits that we need in our 'perfect gundog' to do this work are diverse, and include confidence and boldness (to take on the challenges of varied situations and terrains); speed, style and drive (to make the retrieve quickly, efficiently and in a way that is pleasing to watch); and biddability, calmness and sensibility (because we need the dog to work in partnership with ourselves under our guidance).

Like people, retrievers come in many guises with a variety of temperaments and characters.

Some dogs will have more or fewer of each of these traits, and it is up to us as handlers to bring out the very best in our dogs, and help them to improve in areas that we may consider are weaker.

NURTURING CONFIDENCE

Of the qualities listed above, then, confidence is one of the key factors (just as it is for the handler). Ideally we want a dog that is confident enough to take on new situations with ease, without unfamiliarity affecting its work. We ask our dogs to tackle often difficult terrain or to forge through tough cover and work on their own initiative, sometimes out of sight of their handler. They need to be happy to do this, and also to put their trust in us to guide them when necessary. They should have confidence in themselves and their own ability, but also in us as their handlers. However, we do not want a dog that is so confident that it is bullish and believes that it doesn't need the input from its handler. As with humans, some dogs are more naturally confident

Retrievers require a high degree of confidence to take on unfamiliar obstacles or to work out of sight of their handlers. (Photo: Spencer Morgan)

than others, whereas other dogs will need nurturing to bring out their confidence. An important part of your role as a trainer is to understand the type of dog that you have, and to develop suitable strategies to train it.

Let me tell you a story here, to illustrate how I inadvertently learned a lesson about two of my own dogs' natures from a training exercise. Many years ago I decided I needed to change my commands for casting a dog from a remote static position to the left or right. Having spent my preliminary dog-training years in Zimbabwe, where I picked up American commands that were used there, I was using 'over' with an arm signal to direct a dog both left and right. After training in the UK for a while, I realized that it might be advantageous to use different words to indicate left and right, to enable the dog to understand the difference between the two commands.

So I changed my command for right to 'away' and my command left to 'get on'. And I set about trying to establish this, so that the dog would eventually take the voice-only command for going either left or right without the need for the arm cast as well. I thought this would be useful for rare occasions handling when I was unseen to the dog. The task proved quite a challenge, and my subsequent readings reinforced the fact that dogs have some difficulty with differentiation. This seemed to be the case. As I phased out the arm command gradually and then completely, each dog reacted very differently. I never did succeed in teaching them with 100 per cent certainty to take a voice-only cast left or right, and I decided not to persevere in the end, but I did learn some very valuable information from the exercise about each dog.

THE 'FREEZE' VERSUS THE 'HAVE A GO' DOG

Firstly, this was my experience with my older dog, Pru: when I stopped using the arm movement to cast her and tried with voice only (with no 'body tells' or eye movement as clues), she remained rooted to the spot. This was completely understandable, as she was used to the visual cues of body movement paired with the voice for the cast. Faced with inadequate information, in her mind her best plan was to do nothing so that she didn't get it wrong. This was a reasonable action. However, when I reintroduced the arm signals later, she still wouldn't move! I got the feeling that she felt I had changed the rules so significantly that she no longer understood the game. So she then wasn't confident enough to do anything, and I had to take my time to slowly rebuild her understanding back to where we started.

Bea, on the other hand, in the same scenario, had a go! On my vocal command, every time without fail, she took the cast one way or the other, trying to guess what I wanted and happy just to try something. She got it wrong as many times as she got it right, but that didn't matter to her. Her enthusiasm carried her, and she was undaunted by the changed rules of the game.

So it ended up being a 'fail' in terms of trying to teach them each to cast on a voice command only, but a 'win' in terms of gaining a lot more knowledge about these two dogs. I learnt that Pru was a rule follower and lacked confidence if she didn't receive the information she expected. She was unlikely to rock the status quo. Whereas Bea was a trier: she didn't necessarily know the answers, but she was happy to have a go. She is a keen 'doer' and a rusher.

When you gather information such as this regarding your own individual dog's learning styles, it is invaluable, as it will help you to teach them in a manner that is more appropriate to them. And you can adapt exercises to suit your dog's needs.

THE UNDER-CONFIDENT DOG

For less confident dogs, it is important to help them to believe in themselves and to work on their own initiative. When working on retrieves with this type of dog, put him in a place where he can find the retrieve himself, rather than helping him to pick it. It's a subtle difference, but an important one. All your work with this type of dog should be geared towards making him believe in himself and his own capabilities, and getting him to work more independently.

On marked retrieves, rather than stepping in to help this dog, allow him to work things out for himself. If things go badly wrong and the dog has no hope of picking the retrieve on his own because he has drifted badly out of the area, try calling him in and set up the mark again for him to have another go.

Put the dummy in a place where the dog will find it quickly, once he gets to the correct area.

Regarding memory marks or blinds, set up the exercise for success, so that if the dog takes the initial sendaway or a cast to the area he will 'fall over' a dummy and realize how clever he is to have found it on his own!

With the dog that enjoys being handled, set up situations where he needs to rely on his own initiative a bit more, and try to solve the problem himself. Sometimes try putting yourself out of sight to the dog, to reduce the temptation to intervene. After all, with training, we need to remember it is not about picking the retrieve, but rather teaching the dog. Too often handlers will step in to pick the retrieve with little or no thought about how this is training or improving the dog in front of them.

With both the mark and the blind scenarios, keep in mind what you want and don't change the exercise. That is, if it is a marked retrieve, you want the dog to find the dummy on his own, using his natural ability, and not your control. And with the blind retrieve, you want the dog to take a straight line from your side directly to the area, and handle as needed.

We will look at the ways to do this in more depth in Part Two.

CASE STUDY: RESOLVING EXTREME HANDLER RELIANCE

Background: Three-year-old Labrador Finn had become very 'needy' on all retrieves.

Issue: Finn was relying on Sarah too much to help him find things, and asking questions even on relatively straightforward marks. He had become very 'sticky'. And Sarah had been feeding this habit by giving him help whenever he asked for it.

Action: After watching the dog on a couple of retrieves, I stood Sarah next to a woodshed and threw a large dummy as a mark for Finn. Once she had sent him, I told her to hide behind the woodshed so that if Finn looked back for guidance he wouldn't be able to see her. Sure enough, once Finn reached the rough area of the retrieve he stopped and looked back for Sarah's input and reassurance, but he couldn't see her. He stood still watching for a while, and then decided to move on. He started to hunt and soon found the large dummy.

We repeated this process in short grass with the large dummy that he was able to find quickly, and soon Finn was marking and retrieving more fluidly with no looking back. We then moved on to a smaller dummy, still with the handler out of sight. This meant a more prolonged hunt for Finn, but because he had achieved before in this area, he was gaining confidence all the time. Eventually we were able to move on to a tennis ball, with Finn going to the area and being confident enough to hold his ground without any additional input from Sarah.

Later on, I gave Sarah a marked retrieve for Finn into a dense tree plantation. Once the dog had entered the trees, she could no longer see him and he couldn't see her. This put Sarah out of her comfort zone, as it meant that she couldn't see Finn to help him. She now had to trust him, and he had to rely on himself. I had thrown the mark into an area that I had already 'seeded' with other dummies spaced out on the ground. Finn only had to run to the out-of-sight area and he would find something relatively quickly on his own.

Result: These exercises improved Finn's self-confidence and self-belief. In turn, Sarah began to believe that Finn could get on with the job on his own if need be, and she was less tempted to interfere.

Monkey See, Monkey Do

Another great way for some dogs to gain more confidence is for them to watch other dogs succeeding, and to follow them. Not all dogs will watch other dogs, or learn from them, but some do, and it is a great tool to use to build up confidence in a less confident dog. So, if you have a young dog that is struggling with confidence on long memory marks or blinds, try taking it out with another dog, and let it watch this dog running to the area. If your dog is watching what the other dog is doing, quietly praise her for taking an interest and looking out to the area where the other dog is picking. Then, once the other dog is back, send her to the same area. She is more likely to go out when she has seen another dog be successful and pick from that area. Whilst at a more advanced level you ultimately don't want to encourage 'dog following', this is a very useful tool to help build up confidence in a less confident dog in the early stages of its training.

Stop 'Pushing'

A common tendency in handlers who are trying to bolster confidence in a dog's outrun is to 'shout the dog out' on a retrieve in an attempt to get it to run harder and faster. The misconception is that the louder they shout, the more

With the dog working in thick cover in woodland, the handler has to trust the dog to get on with the job on his own.

Some young dogs benefit from watching another dog succeed on a retrieve, producing a 'monkey see, monkey do' effect.

strongly the dog will go. But this is not the case, and using your voice in this way can just end up pressurizing the dog – and it makes you sound rather desperate, too! Instead, try building confidence through the exercises you are doing, with plenty of memory marks using known areas and visual dummies, and practise keeping your voice soft and upbeat.

Sometimes with a dog that is lacking confidence on these memory marks, increasing its enjoyment of the exercise will really help. Try jogging out to the area where you are going to place the memory mark with the dog, get him excited about the dummy, and then turn round and run back to where you are going to send from. Turn round swiftly to face the memory mark again, but still take a little time to line up the dog carefully, building in some anticipation, then release him with the gentlest of voices. The usual result is that he will fly back with speed as it has all been a great game, and you can praise him vociferously on his outrun to reinforce that what he is doing is right.

THE CONFIDENT DOG

Conversely, for the extremely self-motivated dog, your tactics for approaching retrieves will always be different from those used for the more needy and handler-reliant animal. For example, on a mark you should be looking to handle the headstrong dog periodically, and prove to it that it actually

Speed is desirable for a fast, efficient retrieve, but not at the cost of intelligent gamefinding.

A good memory can be an asset in a retriever after a drive has finished, if it can remember the location of multiple birds.

Sometimes you can watch a dog racing around, taking in a lot of ground with speed and style, but then you realize that he isn't actually going to find anything until he employs his brain more carefully. He is using a lot of effort but very little intelligence to solve the problem. These dogs must be taught to slow themselves down and employ their skills in a more diligently measured and deliberate way.

needs you to help it find, rather than being able to go it alone all the time. You should set out to prove that you are cleverer than the dog.

Most of us – and particularly those who are competing – want a nice helping of style and drive in our dogs. It makes them a pleasure to watch working, whether that is taking a line on a runner or powering out swiftly on an unseen retrieve. Pace is definitely important. We want our dogs to reach the area quickly and efficiently. But don't confuse 'rushing' with drive.

The Clever Dog

Having a clever dog is a double-edged sword! With a gundog, we want them to do what they are told and go where we point them, to fetch that unseen retrieve. We want them to take our directions obediently, and not question them or problem solve independently, but once they get to the area of the retrieve we then want them to

Field Trial Champion Jobeshill Octavia (Pru) with her light eyes! (Photo: Caroline Dell)

switch on that initiative and use their skills to find the bird themselves. It is forever a fine balancing act between working on handler direction and working with their own innate abilities. And some dogs will naturally be more inclined one way than the other.

There are dogs that are extremely biddable and just want to hang on our every word, and do what we ask – these dogs will often 'lean' on us for more guidance than we would actually like. And there are others that are somewhat more self-interested or motivated, and who take on too much initiative – always trying to get ahead of the curve and take matters into their own hands. The ideal situation would be a mix of both, of course.

The clever dog often comes with a great memory. And it is very rewarding when the dog remembers a long-down mark and powers back for it without further command – as long as it remembers the one that you intended! Sometimes having a not-so-clever dog, which just does what you ask rather than trying to overthink the situation, is actually more of a bonus, particularly in those drive scenarios where multiple birds are down.

UNDER PRESSURE

As kind and 'reward-based' as we think our training is for our gundogs, there will always be a notion of pressure, too. Whilst the activity of retrieving is rewarding, we are asking the dog to do this on our terms – when we want, how we want. This in itself is a form of pressure. We are telling the dog to go and do this now, not when they might feel like it, or in the way they might want to do it. Often we require the dog to take the most direct route to a retrieve, which is not necessarily the easiest one for him. So we require retrieving done, but on our terms. On the whole, though, if you train in a positive way, you will minimize pressure for the dog, because the rewards will outweigh any negative feelings.

I was once told by a very high-profile trainer to get rid of my dog because it had light eyes, and in his experienced opinion, light-eyed Labradors were not able to put up with the pressure of competing successfully in field trials. Being naïve and stubborn, I persevered with my dog (I didn't have a replacement option), and was gratified to make her into my first Field Trial Champion. In my mind, I felt that she wouldn't need to cope with any pressure, as that was not the way I trained. I didn't use any pressure in my training methods to achieve my goals.

However, as I later found out, the dog can feel pressure from other sources, and not just from the handler. For example, in group training, just as a handler can feel under pressure from their training companions, so too can the dog feel pressure from the group situation. This could be

CASE STUDY: KITTY, LINING TO MEMORY BLINDS

This young puppy was clearly extremely clever, right from the start, and I was able to move along very quickly with her training as she picked up new concepts with ease. But in the early stages of teaching her to go out on blinds, through memory work, I over-complicated things with the use of distractions, and this resulted in a shut-down from her. When I put my arm out to line her up and cue her to run, instead of getting ready to go she actually reversed a couple of steps and sat down! My arm signal in her mind had come to represent a form of pressure, rather than anticipation and enjoyment. We had reached a hiatus. At this point I had a very promising dog that could handle nicely, hunt beautifully and stop, but she just wouldn't go!

I had to take some remedial steps to build back trust and confidence into our send away position. I backtracked my training to treat her as a very young puppy again. And I made the sendaway the most pleasurable part of her day by dividing her breakfast or dinner into three separate bowls. I showed her the food bowl, left her side and walked out with it for about fifteen to twenty metres, then returned to her. I then lined her up with all the usual cues for a blind retrieve, and sent her to the food bowl. I repeated this several times from the same position, then from a different position, and then later on with pre-planted food bowls that she could see from where she was sitting.

These simple activities helped to restore her confidence and enjoyment in the lining set-up, as they were highly rewarding and separated out just the outrun part of the full retrieve sequence. We were then able to move forwards to work on short visible memory blinds to a white target dummy. Gradually her trust and understanding was rebuilt, and we progressed again slowly from there.

Lining towards a white 'target' dummy that the dog can see clearly to build or restore confidence.

the sheer number of people, when the dog finds it daunting to return to the line or its handler as it is facing a 'sea of people'. I call this 'line pressure', and it can manifest itself in slow returns to the handler, or issues with the retrieve (such as the dog putting down or mouthing a dummy or bird).

Another example of group pressure is when the dog is asked to run down the front of the line of handlers and dogs, to a retrieve off the end of the line. Passing in such close proximity to other dogs can be daunting for a young and inexperienced dog, and you will sometimes see these dogs 'banana' across the front of the line to reach the retrieve.

Finally, the dog may also pick up on the group vibe. If there is a lot of shouting or tension during training, a sensitive dog may react to this and feel pressure. If your neighbour's dog keeps running in, and he shouts at it each time, you shouldn't be surprised if your dog is more reluctant to go out there himself. Just as for humans, there is the potential for your dog to experience feelings of pressure all around, and sensitive treatment of the group situation is needed to acclimatize him in a positive way to this.

And even with training in a reward-based way, if things get too complicated, or you move along too fast in your teaching, or the dog becomes confused, again the dog can feel this as a form of pressure. Some years ago I encountered this problem in the early stages of training of a particularly bright young bitch, Kitty, when I overcomplicated things, and this resulted in her shutting down (see box).

Running down the line of guns and field trial competitors, back towards the handler and a gallery of spectators, can be unnerving for an inexperienced novice dog. (Photo: Caroline Dell)

4 APPROACHES TO TRAINING

A gem cannot be polished without friction, nor a man perfected without trials.

Attributed to the Roman philosopher Seneca

It is nearly one hundred years since *The Practical Breaking and Training of Gundogs* was written by C. Mackay Sanderson (1922), and since then dog-training methods have moved on considerably. However, in some instances gundog trainers have been slower to catch up with the more positive, reward-based motivational methods that are now mainstream in many other dog sports.

Training methods from just a few decades ago relied on handlers dominating their gundogs in an attempt to show them who the 'alpha' or leader of the pack was, and harsh punishments were not uncommon when dogs failed to toe the line in their owners' eyes. Nowadays, modern dog trainers do not rely on dominating a dog or forcing it to do something, but rather on a relationship based on trust, where handler and dog work together in partnership.

A WOLF IN DOG'S CLOTHING?

These archaic domination methods sprang from the belief that dogs are descendants of wolves, and as such a 'pack theory' must relate to them. It is true that dogs have virtually the same mitochondrial DNA as wolves, as well as the same number of chromosomes and the same number of teeth. They are also highly social animals. But during their long evolution a lot of changes took place to form the *Canis familiaris* – today's pet dog.

The dog's brain is a lot smaller than that of a wolf, and it has changed, because its priorities are no longer the same as a wolf. Wolves have to concern themselves with survival, hunting to eat, and reproduction, whereas the domestic dog's needs revolve mainly around finding pleasure or reward in his environment. Dogs no longer have the predatory instincts to survive alone in the wild without the help of humans. And whereas wolf bitches come into season, to reproduce, only once a year so that her pups are born in the spring, the domestic dog is more likely to have two seasons a year at any time. The differences don't stop there. The appearance of the modern dog in its myriad of breeds has altered, in some cases beyond recognition, from the wolf.

Furthermore, the premise that wolves live in hierarchical packs with an 'alpha' male is factually incorrect. The pack theory was based largely upon research undertaken in the 1940s (Schenkel 1947), which observed captive wolves that were forced together as unrelated individuals living in a zoo. Forming hierarchies was their way of dealing with being thrown together in an unnatural, captive situation. Schenkel didn't include any study of wolves in the wild, and his studies remained the main resource on the social behaviour of wolves for many years. However, more recent work spent time studying wolves in the wild (Mech 1999) found that they actually live in family units much like our own, with two parents along with their offspring.

Various dog-training books and trainers have suggested that dogs need 'alphas', in the same way that wolves supposedly did, and that humans should establish themselves as the 'pack leader' over their canine charges. But many of these theories of dominance and subordination have now been largely debunked, or at least deeply discredited. And as Ian Dunbar said in an interview with Louise Rafkin for the *San Francisco Chronicle* (October 2006), it makes as much sense to think that wolves can teach us how to interact with our dogs, as it does to suggest that reviewing chimps' behaviour will help us inform

Above and below: The diminutive Dachshund and the noble Bracco Italiano bear little resemblance to their early ancestor the wolf.

Research shows that wild wolves live in family groups rather than hierarchical packs. (Photo: George Howard)

our own parenting skills.

Dogs have evolved to live with, and alongside humans, and to fit into our social interactions. As such, a family hierarchy is much more applicable to their status and needs. So perhaps dogs need 'parents' rather than pack leaders? Certainly the family structure, which sets limits and examples, does teach members how to behave in a socially acceptable way, with a system of manners and respect for other group members – the mother and father rule. Being the 'calm grown-up' with our canine charges is a more relevant way forwards than trying to be some sort of alpha.

This leads on to where the dog should live – the great kennel debate. Some believe that life in a kennel makes the gundog more willing to work with you, as it has limited access to human interaction. The feeling is that a dog kept outside, away from day-to-day family interactions, will be more attentive. Others prefer their dogs to live with them as part of the family in the house. There is no single correct answer. Do what works for you and your family situation.

At Stauntonvale we have dogs in the house, as well as dogs in outside kennels. We use a kennel for practical reasons, because we have several

Kennels make practical sense if you have multiple dogs.

dogs and not enough 'house space' for them all. But we often bring the 'kennel' dogs indoors to lie on the sofa with us, and enjoy watching us prepare and eat dinner! I have made up a Field Trial Champion that lived solely in the house, and now sleeps on our bed, and I've made up others that spent the majority of their time in the kennel. Where the dog sleeps shouldn't make a difference to how they relate to you and how they train, as long as you maintain some 'house rules'.

APPLYING SCIENCE TO BEHAVIOUR

Behavioural science has its roots in the laboratory work of the 1800s. Behaviourists concerned themselves with studying actual observable behaviour, rather than the mind and emotions. In the 1930s, B. F. Skinner developed this work and proposed that to understand behaviour we have to look at its causes, and in turn the consequences. This is what he called 'operant conditioning', and it is a method of learning that

Labradors happily adapt to most living environments!

comes about through reward and punishment, where the subject makes a positive or negative association between particular behaviours and their consequences (Skinner 1938).

Skinner believed that it was more productive to study actual behaviour than thought and the mental state. He conducted experiments, notably on rats that he placed in a 'Skinner box'. He found that he could change the behaviour of rats by giving them a food reward for pressing a lever. The rats soon learnt that pressing the lever led to them receiving food, so they repeated the action. From these experiments Skinner noted that behaviour that was followed by pleasant consequences was likely to be repeated, whereas behaviour followed by an unpleasant experience was less likely to be repeated. He introduced the term 'reinforcer', meaning that reinforced behaviour is strengthened, whereas behaviour that is not reinforced will be weakened or extinguished.

Skinner also noted that punishment, being the opposite of reinforcement, weakened behaviour. It was aversive. Punishment can be applied either directly, such as administering an electric shock, or indirectly by removing a privilege. However, there are some major problems associated with using punishment in training. For example, punishment can have a lasting effect and can cause fear and loss of confidence. Also, punishment does not guide the subject towards the desired behaviour. It only provides the 'what not to do' part of the picture. And, whilst punishment may suppress behaviour at the time, once the punishment is no longer present, the behaviour will quickly return. Using aversives can affect your relationship with your dog, erode trust and degrade your bond. So, using punishment should be done with extreme caution.

Relating the use of reinforcers to training, my dogs understand that they will receive praise or a food treat if they exhibit a behaviour that I want. If they are doing something that I don't want, this will be ignored, or I will use a vocal interrupter to avert the behaviour, such as 'ah, ah' or 'no' (vocal 'punishment') or a non-reward marker, such as 'try again'.

PRIMARY VERSUS SECONDARY REINFORCERS

For the rats in Skinner's box, food was the primary reinforcer. Primary reinforcers are things that are innately rewarding, such as food, sex, touch, play. They occur naturally and don't need to be learned. If you reward your dog with a food treat for sitting on cue, this is primary reinforcement.

Secondary reinforcers, on the other hand, need to be associated with a primary reinforcer for them to have any effect. Verbal praise is a secondary reinforcer. The words themselves have no inherent value of their own. For example, saying 'good boy' to your dog would be meaningless unless it was previously associated with the pleasure of receiving a loving stroke or a food treat. The secondary reinforcement has to be conditioned.

Most people have heard of Russian physiologist Ivan Pavlov's (1902) experiments with dogs, which became conditioned to salivate at the sound of a bell because they had been fed immediately after hearing somebody ring a bell repeatedly. The dogs learnt the association between the bell and food, and came to expect food when they heard the bell ring, eventually salivating whether the food was offered or not. The response is known as a 'conditioned response', or sometimes a Pavlovian response, whereby a previously neutral stimulus has become a conditioned stimulus. This is an example of secondary reinforcement.

Likewise for humans, money is a secondary reinforcer. Money itself, as paper notes or metal coins, does not have any intrinsically rewarding qualities, but it can be used to acquire the primary reinforcers that we might crave, such as new clothes, food or pleasurable experiences.

When we look at using reinforcers in our training, we need to be aware that not all reinforcers are equal. Some will hold more value over others. So if we are walking our dog at heel in the training field and want it to trot along attentively with its head up, we need to be aware that our mediocre secondary reinforcer of a vocal 'good boy' might not be as rewarding as the primary reinforcement provided by ground-sniffing that he would rather indulge in. The ground-sniffing is satisfying a strong biological need.

The advantage of using secondary reinforcement is that it allows the trainer to deliver rein-

CLICKER TRAINING

In recent years, dog trainers have adopted the use of a clicker as a secondary reinforcer.

This 'modern' technique of using a clicker as a reward marker and to shape behaviours in a dog, actually has its roots back in the 1950s and 1960s, in the sphere of marine animal training. Keller Breland, a student of B. F. Skinner, and his wife Marian (Breland & Breland 1951), developed the first operant-based marine mammal shows in the USA, using a conditioned reinforcer, in this case a whistle. The whistle was used to inform the dolphin that he had earned a fish for performing a desired behaviour. In the 1990s, other animal trainers started using operant conditioning, conditioned reinforcers, shaping techniques and positive reinforcement, and it wasn't long before the general public followed suit, using a metal clicker contained in a plastic casing as a conditioned reinforcer for their dog's behaviour. Clicker training was born.

The concept behind clicker training is that the 'click' is used to mark the precise time that a desired behaviour is performed. For example, if a dog places its paw on a platform the trainer would click the dog for this behaviour and reward the dog. If the dog doesn't place its paw on the platform, or offers some other sort of behaviour, there are no negative consequences, the dog

forcement even when the dog doesn't have a particular biological need at that moment. It is a form of bridging technology that indicates that the subject has done right, and that a reward will follow.

Young retrievers being trained using the clicker for some of their foundation obedience work.

just doesn't receive the click and the subsequent reward. There is no 'fear factor' that can be associated with punishment or negative consequences of behaviour. Consequently, the clicker is a valuable tool for helping animals to innovate. This is why the clicker method was so useful with marine animals, as the dolphins often offered novel and unusual behaviours in an attempt to win a reward. They were uninhibited, and happy to try things to find new ways of being rewarded.

This was ideal with marine mammals that were used to performing displays, as it often gave the trainers exciting and unexpected new routines. But for training gundogs, we don't really want our dogs to innovate, or to go through a range of behaviours before eventually alighting on the desired behaviour. So, whilst the clicker is a timely feedback mechanism for our dogs (a reward marker), it only provides them with half a picture: *you did that bit right.*

Clicker trainers use the clicker to shape behaviour through tiny incremental steps. For example, if the eventual desired outcome is for a dog to hold a ball in its mouth, in the early stages the clicker trainer will click the dog for just looking at the ball. Then they will move the bar slightly to offer a click when the dog moves towards the ball. Then they will only offer a click when the dog places his nose on the ball, and then puts his mouth on the ball, and so on and so on, until the dog eventually picks up the ball and holds it in his mouth. The process of getting there may have taken some time and many, many sessions, and the dog may have exhibited a lot of other behaviours that were not desired or unproductive.

Clicker training can be useful for training some of the basic gundog obedience behaviours, but it requires some manual dexterity to operate the clicker in one hand, treat delivery in the other, and possibly hold a lead, too. It can sometimes feel slow because the dog is only receiving feedback on some of its behaviour. So I prefer to link this method to the use of a 'non-reward' marker as well, to give feedback to the dog when they are not close to receiving a reward. I don't use a negative tone, as I don't want to inhibit the dog. I usually say 'try again'. I just want to help the dog acknowledge that there won't be a reward for that particular offered behaviour, so he can stop trying it in vain. This tends to speed up the process of learning, as it marks the unsuccessful behaviour, feeding back to the dog that it isn't the way forwards to gain a reward. It encourages them to try another direction.

Instead of using a clicker, you can use your voice as a vocal marker (or event marker) with a 'good boy/girl' at the precise moment that you like what you see. I do this, as I don't have a clicker in every jacket or bag, but I always have my voice. As long as you are disciplined and consistent with the delivery of the secondary reinforcer 'good boy', then you can get much the same effect that you would using a clicker. It is very much about timing, in that you have to mark the behaviour at the precise instant that it is correct and what you want, otherwise you may end up inadvertently marking something that you don't desire.

For example, you want to praise a dog on his strong return with the dummy as he is racing back towards you – but just as you deliver the praise he has begun rolling and mouthing the dummy as he returns. Therefore the dog may associate your praise with playing with the dummy in his mouth. You need to be extremely vigilant to ensure that what you are reinforcing is what you actually want, and also that the dog understands why he is receiving reinforcement.

COMMUNICATE AND MOTIVATE

For your dog to respond to you, you need to communicate what you want him to do, and provide him with adequate motivation for doing so. You need both factors. If one is not there, or inadequate, you will reduce the chance of success. The reinforcers you offer need to be great enough. For example, in the case above where the dog is walking at heel but keeps ground-sniffing, the praise being offered when his head is not on the floor is not enough to outweigh the distraction of game scent on the ground (and the reinforce-

Ground-sniffing interesting game scents can prove more positively reinforcing for a young dog than walking to heel with the head up.

63

ment he is getting from sniffing it). He is unlikely to comply. You will need to 'up' the reward or improve your relationship with the dog so that you become more interesting and exciting.

Chosen reinforcers and your relationship with the dog need to outweigh the distractors and aversive stimuli present in the environment (for example, vocal praise/food treat plus your bond, keeps the dog walking attentively at heel). Over time, the dog will come to learn that great things come from being with you: food, play, and access to retrieves.

Be consistent in the feedback that you give your dog for its behaviour.

THE ABC OF DOG TRAINING

We know that reinforcers are likely to strengthen behaviour, and that punishment will weaken behaviour, but we now need to add in the cue or command that precedes the behaviour to get the full sequence of events. Skinner's theory of operant conditioning used the following three terms: stimulus, response and reinforcement. But it is also commonly known as ABC – Antecedent, Behaviour, Consequence – by behaviour analysts. This term gives us an easy-to-remember structure to relate to our own retriever-training process.

For example:

Antecedent = The trainer commands the dog to sit
Behaviour = The dog sits
Consequence = The trainer gives the dog a sausage

So, A is giving a command (stimulus), B is what the dog does in response to the command (in this case the choice is binary: he sits, or doesn't sit), and C will be either a reward for a sit, or no reward or punishment for not sitting.

ABC gives students a really clear way of looking at what they are asking of their dogs, and how they are learning. It is a systematic approach, which can be broken down clearly into the component parts, and gives the trainer a framework for feedback to and communication with the dog.

This method provides a very black and white view of behaviour, and lays down guidelines in simple terms that a dog (and its handler) can understand. It can be used to mark right behaviour or wrong behaviour. However, it doesn't really deal with not-quite-right behaviour, so what do we do about that? My late mentor Dave Probert had a famous saying: 'Nearly right is wrong!' If we look at that in relation to the example above, and our dog 'hovers' rather than fully sits, we should classify this as wrong (it's a 'no-sit'), and not the outcome we were wanting or expecting. We would give feedback to the dog that that is not what is required, and the dog would only gain the reward as a consequence of sitting firmly. That seems obvious.

Where things start to get muddied, for the dog more than the handler, is when you start to accept undesirable behaviours, or behaviours that are nearly right but not quite what you want. You 'let things go'. For example, in a group lesson you notice that your dog is slightly further forward in the heel position than you would want. There are quite a few people in the group, and you are feeling rather jaded, so you carry on and ignore the poor heelwork, and in turn give the dog a retrieve when it is your go. As far as the dog is concerned, then, everything is good. He hasn't had any feedback to suggest otherwise, so he safely assumes that his new slightly forward heel position is acceptable, and he's had several rewarding retrieves to reinforce this.

On the following day, he behaves in exactly the same way, but this time you have decided that you are not going to accept this. The dog is surprised that on Tuesday the behaviour he exhibited was considered good, and on Wednesday when he exhibited the same behaviour it was considered bad! He ends up being quite confused. And there is no learning to be taken out of the situation for him, other than it being a different day of the week or a different location. You have been unfair on the dog, tolerating something on one day and then not on the next. To aid learning, then, you need to be consistent in what you reinforce for the dog, and in your feedback about what you think about his behaviour. This will give him consistent information from which to learn.

Dogs learn by succeeding and being rewarded, but conversely the occasional mistake or non-required behaviour, where they don't receive any reinforcement, or where they receive a positive punishment (such as a vocal interrupter or correction), will also aid learning. For example, the dog that makes a noise due to excitement when a shot is fired and a dummy is thrown, will be denied the retrieve until he is quiet. If this is applied consistently, he will soon learn the pattern that he is only sent when he remains quiet and calm, and is never sent if he makes a noise.

BEHAVIOUR CHAINS

We have looked at behaviour and response as solo elements, and this is of use when we break down tasks in training. Many of the obedience skills are simple single-step processes – for example, asking for 'sit', and then praising the dog for sitting. However, as we progress into retrieving, we find these foundation elements are woven into more complex chains of behaviour. For example, the seemingly straightforward basic marked retrieve actually comprises the following behaviours from the dog: he must

- remain steady and quiet at heel until told to retrieve
- ignore distractions
- mark the fall of the retrieve item
- run out to the area on handler cue
- on arrival at the fall area, hunt to locate the retrieve
- pick up the retrieve item
- return directly towards the handler, carrying the retrieve
- deliver the retrieve to hand

It is a technical chain of events, where each behaviour in turn sets the occasion for the next one – for example, the dog cannot deliver to hand without having first located and picked up the retrieve item. Unlike in other dog sports, such as agility, the individual elements in the chain are not each handler cued, but are cued by the behaviours that precede them – for example, picking up the retrieve cues the direct return to the handler. It is an organized string of events, where each response in the chain becomes the stimulus for the next sequence of behaviour.

Chains of behaviour can provide gundog trainers with problems both in their correct maintenance – keeping good chains – but also in accidentally creating chains that are not desired. One example, as we cited above, is the dog that collects the retrieve but afterwards continues to hunt on with the dummy in his mouth. The handler, who does not see the dog hunting on as it is obscured by cover, vocally praises the dog just after he picks the retrieve (in his mind praising the find), but the dog understands the praise to be linked to precisely what it was doing at that point – hunting on – and it has now been positively reinforced for this undesirable activity. It is likely that this chain of behaviour will be repeated because it was reinforced, not only by the handler offering praise, but because the act of hunting itself was positively reinforcing for the dog.

Having an understanding of behaviour chains will help you, as a trainer, to deal with issues as they arrive. To strengthen weak areas in your training, practise individual elements of a behaviour chain, before linking them back into the chain. Teach each skill and build fluency in it, and then reassemble the chain. Remember, there must be sufficient reinforcement of the behaviours to maintain the sequence. If things go wrong in your behaviour chain, look at what could be influencing this, such as external influencers or reinforcers.

There are three ways of approaching chains of behaviour:

Complete task chaining: The dog must do the entire chain before receiving any reward. (For example, the dog does a difficult blind retrieve and the handler rewards the dog on completion with a fun throw of his favourite toy.)

Forward chaining: You start at the front of the chain and teach each skill separately, reinforcing each successful step in the sequence. (An example might be a retrieve over a fence into thick cover, where the handler teaches the dog to jump the fence first, rewarding that behaviour, and then progresses to teaching the dog to hunt an area of cover to find the retrieve, again rewarding that behaviour.)

Back-chaining: You ask for the final behaviour, and then ask for the behaviour before it as well, and then the one before that. For example, working on delivery of a retrieve, the handler asks for a static hold of the dummy, with the dog sitting in front of them. Once that is mastered, he then adds a recall on, with the dog sitting remotely with the dummy in his mouth and then returning to present the dummy. Next the handler can ask the dog to recall, pick the dummy on the in-run, and then present. And finally, the handler can link the outrun back on to the sequence.

CHOICE-BASED TRAINING

Having reviewed the role of positive reinforcement in training, we can see how dogs learn through rewarding their behaviour, and giving feedback on it, and how communication can play an important role in this teaching process. But we can also aid understanding by letting dogs make choices for themselves so they learn from their own actions.

For example, when I am teaching a handler with a young dog that is still not fully steady, I will ask the handler to take their dog off the lead and settle it at heel. At this point they usually look extremely concerned, knowing that their dog is likely to run in. Before I have even thrown a dummy, the handler has said 'stay, stay, stay' to his dog, and is holding a hand up in front of the dog's face like a policeman, and standing in a very uptight and tense way – all of which is giving the dog information. So I will say to the handler: 'One command and then put your hands by your sides and relax. What's the worst that can happen?' The handler normally admits 'He will run in' – to which I reply 'So?' They look at me slightly aghast, as if this doesn't even bear contemplating. But I explain that when the dog runs in I will pick up the dummy. That is all that will happen – no shouting, no recriminations. The dummy will simply disappear, so the dog will get nothing as a result of his efforts.

I throw the dummy, and sure enough the dog runs in. I pick up the dummy, and the dog gets up to the fall to find nothing there. The handler calls the dog back and settles him back in position. We repeat the process, and every time the dog runs in, I just pick up the dummy. The dog never retrieves the dummy and therefore never gets any reward for running in. We re-set him. After a few more attempts the dog gives up running in. We repeat the throw. The dog remains steady, and the handler then uses a vocal command to send the dog. The dog has learned that only by sitting or standing calmly will he be sent to retrieve the dummy, which is the reward he desires.

The dog has gone wrong several times, but achieved no reward. The reward only came when he exhibited the right behaviour. This method will only work if you have somebody else to pick up the dummy for you, so that the dog can't self-reward when he runs in.

The handler in this situation has not provided any direct feedback or vocal communication to the dog on his behaviour – the learning has

A dog that repeatedly 'runs in' but never gets to retrieve the dummy will soon work out how to achieve success through changing his behaviour.

come from the dog working out the pattern for himself, and understanding what he must do to achieve the reward.

PAPERING OVER THE CRACKS

The handler above who has to say 'stay' multiple times and use body language to hold the dog in position or stop it running in, is masking the symptoms of a potential issue. By using several commands and body-blocking, they are preventing their dog from running in, and they have no idea if the dog would be steady without these commands – although they have a fairly good idea that he won't be. But they will only find out if the dog is steady once they get into a 'test' situation, either in competition or in the field.

The same goes for the handler who puts in a recall as soon as his dog has picked the dummy from a place where there are multiple dummies.

The reason he does this is in case the dog decides to swap, or to stop it swapping. But how do we know the dog was going to swap? What does it do if you don't put in the recall? You won't know in this situation unless you give it a chance. You don't know if the dog had it in his mind to swap before he heard the recall whistle, or whether he had no intention of swapping anyway. My point is that you want to go into a competition or into the shooting field *knowing* that your dog won't swap when there is a temptation of multiple retrieves on offer. So if you don't put in the recall, and it swaps, then you know that you have an issue to deal with, and you can properly address this in a separate training exercise at a later date.

The wallpaper protagonists will say that putting in the whistle encourages a good habit, and there is some logic in that, if you look at it in terms of building 'muscle memory'. But my point is that,

When the dog reaches an area of multiple dummies, allow it to decide what it should do next and then provide feedback on that behaviour.

also knows that that is what earns him the reward of the retrieve. Both you and your dog are comfortable, as you know and understand the cues to gaining the reward. If you don't allow problems to be manifested, then you will never know how effective your training is, and how the dog will behave when he is out of sight and under his own volition. Training is your opportunity to improve the dog for the future.

In this respect, consider how you handle during training, and treat it differently to how you might handle during a competition. In training, you are under no pressure to pick the retrieve. You merely set up the retrieves as an opportunity to train the dog, and you should be concerning yourself with *how* you pick them, rather than just picking them. Conversely, in working tests and field trials you are being judged on picking the retrieve as best you can. When things go wrong, you sometimes have to battle on to pick the retrieve at all costs. The two approaches are fundamentally different.

conversely, the dog may be relying on hearing the whistle before it comes back, as part of its muscle-memory routine. You want the dog to fill its mouth and then automatically speed back without having to wait for the cue of a recall whistle. Furthermore, what will you do when the dog is out of sight and picking in a similar circumstance, where there are known to be multiple retrieves? If you cannot see the dog, then you have no idea when he has filled his mouth and when to recall him. However, if you have rehearsed not using a whistle in a multi-dummy pick situation, and he is coming back straightaway without hearing the whistle, then you can feel a lot more confident that he is going to pick and return to his handler even when he is out of sight.

By allowing your dog to make choices in training, and providing him with feedback on these choices, you are ensuring that you know how the dog will behave in these circumstances. It is better to deal with problems when you have an opportunity in training, rather than trying to cover them up with additional behaviour and cues. For example, you want your dog to choose to maintain his heel position because he sees it as a good place to be, where he gets rewarded. He waits calmly at heel, but focused on the retrieve, because he

ATTRITION IN TRAINING

Another method that can be of use in some instances in gundog training is the use of 'attrition': that is, reissuing a command until the dog takes it on board. This is not the same as just repeating a command. The dictionary definition implies a process of grinding down: 'The process of reducing something's strength or effectiveness through sustained attack or pressure' (*The Oxford English Dictionary*). But it is not that the dog is being worn down, but rather its resistance to the suggested command. This is not to be confused with nagging.

Attrition is a process of allowing other behaviours, without punishing or correcting them, but bringing the dog back to what you originally stated each time. For example, if you try to cast the dog left to the dummy (into the wind) and the dog peels back, instead of vocally chastising him, you stop him, recall him to the spot where he was originally, stop him, and recast him left. Again, he pulls back. You stop him, recall him, stop him and recast him left again. Each time the dog is not taking the command, but he is not actually making any progress by it, as you are bringing him back to the place where he received the initial command. He hasn't gained any ground in the direction he was favouring, so his behaviour is not getting him anywhere. Eventually he takes the original left-hand cast and picks the retrieve – the learning being that if he listens to his handler he will get the reward.

Attrition can be a useful method with a sensitive dog (as long as he is whistle tolerant) where you don't want to vocally correct, as it may have a negative effect, and where you can't use choice-based training options because there is a risk that the dog may self-reward.

We will look at specific examples of how and when these different training approaches can be applied in Part Two. Some will have more relevance in particular situations, or with certain types of dog.

PART TWO: POWER

5 START INDOORS

Advanced Retriever Training is intended very much as a 'follow on' book to some of the more preliminary or introductory manuals on gundog training. As such, it will not be reiterating elementary information found in most of those books (that is, puppy choice and naming, toilet training, basic training equipment and commands, innoculations and so on). It is assumed that most readers will have a good working knowledge of their chosen breed already, and in many instances will be training their second or additional gundog, or living in a multi-dog household.

However, there are some basic elements that are worth dwelling on, because they form such an important foundation for advanced retriever training. It cannot be stated enough that doing the basics, getting the groundwork right, is so important. If you don't do that, your whole 'house' will crumble.

RELATIONSHIPS, ROUTINES AND RESPECT

When people ask for advice concerning training issues with very young puppies, especially on internet forums and social media, you will often hear the response 'Just let it be a puppy'. But what does that actually mean? Surely not just letting it run feral, with no rules or basic training? Some people seem to take the view that a puppy should remain untouched, a blank canvas, for later work when it reaches the age of about eight to twelve months. But by doing this, you are missing out on vital time when the puppy is impressionable and easy to mould into the sort of family member that you would eventually

want. If you draw an analogy with a young child, you wouldn't leave that to its own devices in its early years. Instead, you would concentrate on letting it retain its childhood, having fun time and building your bond together, but within fair and consistent guidelines. You would teach rules and manners, and in turn the child would learn to trust you and respect your relationship.

A similar nanny or patient parent approach to a young pup is probably the best one. Start as you mean to go on. I always work on the premise that it is much easier to build a good habit than break a bad one. And with the young pup in the house, there are so many training opportunities that just arise naturally as part of its normal day. The pup need never know that it is actually being trained. For example, meal times (three or four times a day) afford the ideal opportunity to instil some routines regarding manners, basic obedience commands and patience. Having time with the puppy indoors means that you can set boundaries and be fair in reinforcing them kindly.

Starting an eight-week-old pup in the house, using crate training when it can't be supervised, also makes toilet training very straightforward. It quickly establishes a routine and structure to the young dog's day, and it will also learn the 'house rules' and respect for other members of the family (human and canine). This way, ground rules are laid down early, giving a solid foundation from which to build. I usually keep my own pups in the house until they are around seven to eight months, depending on the time of year. This means they are fully toilet trained and clean in the kennel when they finally go outside. For some people this is not necessary, but our dogs

71

Keeping a young puppy indoors can help it learn how to interact with all family members, and also learn the rules of the house.

relationship with your dog, strengthening your bond, and creating a well-mannered shooting companion for the future.

In these early weeks and months, with the puppy indoors, you can also fit small snippets of training around daily routines and chores. So, for example, while cooking dinner, try a few sits or some steps of heelwork. For me, part of the enjoyment of having working gundogs is having their companionship within our family. It works for us to have them in the house, and is most of the joy of gundog ownership. This early conditioning, when the puppy is very young and impressionable, is very straightforward but can really bolster your later training, particularly with reference to the stop whistle. If you have used it as part of your routine to sit and look at you before dinner, the response becomes virtually Pavlovian further down the line – it doesn't occur to my dogs not to stop when they hear the whistle later on in their schooling in the field,

spend time both in the house and kennel, so it is useful that they are clean in both.

Having the young puppy indoors means that I have plenty of time to find out about its personality through observation and play. Being around the pup for the majority of the time gives me more knowledge of its nature and drivers, and insight into how to go about its early training. My approach is to work with the dog in front of me, and so I look at what I have got and train that brain. One size certainly doesn't fit all, and although I have my own methods (along with most trainers), I always look at adapting and tailoring my style for each individual puppy that we have. I can honestly say that we have not had two puppies that have been the same, although in recent years they have all been related to each other.

Basic obedience behaviours – sits, stays, recalls and early heelwork (we will look at this in depth in the next chapter) – are the core skills you will be teaching your young retriever puppy in these first few months of its life. Keep the training appropriate, and reward good work with praise, play and treats. All this will help you build your

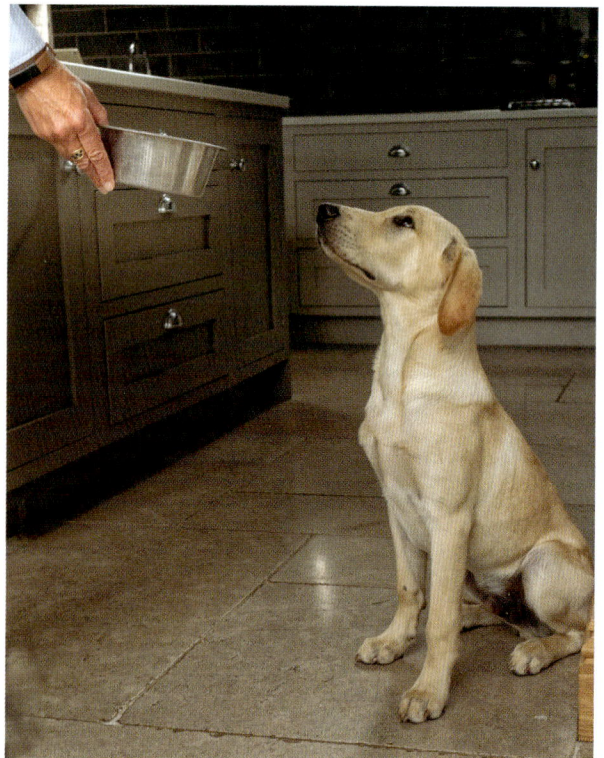

Meal times are a good opportunity for some basic obedience training.

as it has been effectively conditioned into them from an early age. The decision-making process has been removed from them.

RIGHT FIRST TIME

In all your early foundation work, you should be thinking about 'practising success'. By this I mean, ensuring that if you are using a command, then the puppy is already carrying out the desired activity. In this respect, never call a puppy if you don't think there is a 100 per cent chance that it will come towards you. Instead, wait until you get that forward motion towards you, by moving away from it quickly as it catches your eye, and then add in the recall command as it starts to chase towards you. In this way the puppy has done a successful recall that can now be rewarded. In addition, it has not learnt that a recall command can be ignored, with sometimes greater gain (sniffing something satisfying on the ground). By promoting the desired behaviour first, before adding a command to it, you will give the young puppy every opportunity to get all its commands right.

In the unfortunate circumstance that you do issue a command and the puppy does not respond to it, never be tempted to repeat the command. Go and collect the puppy, or ignore it and walk away to do something else. Try to operate on a once-and-once-only basis, as this is what you will want your dog to work to in the future. If you give two commands and later more, the dog will learn that you will just call it again, or repeat the command, and that it isn't necessary for it to relate to the first command. In this way you will considerably weaken the meaning of your command.

TEACHING PATIENCE

The use of a crate (large cage) as a safe place and bed for when the pup cannot be supervised in the home is ideal. Spending some time in the crate, at times out of sight of you or the family, will accustom the pup to being alone and settling down, relaxed in its own company, and will avoid any potential issue of separation anxiety in later life.

A very important part of conditioning the young gundog is building in 'frustration tolerance' whereby the pup must learn to control its impulses and show restraint. Teaching a 'wait' or 'stay' command before it is released from the crate, or from the back of the car, teaches the young, impetuous puppy to be patient in order to gain a reward. It is learning that good things come to those who wait, which will be of great relevance in its later gundog career. The pup has to understand that it cannot obtain instant gratification, which it initially did when its dam fed it as part of the litter.

I don't go to the lengths of some trainers, such as Jan Fennell (2002), who suggest making the dog wait while you go through a door first, to teach it some sort of pecking order. For me, it is the act of waiting, rather than the concept of rank, that is the important part in these types of exercise.

Teaching young dogs to deal with frustration is a key consideration in building towards a quiet and steady young gundog in the field. Frustration comes from the inability to control an outcome, and the lack of a shared common language, in which the puppy can adequately express itself. If we can teach our puppies to 'ask' us for things by displaying the behaviours we are after, their lives will become less frustrating and more rewarding. For example, a young pup that sits and then looks up at his owner will gain the reward of praise, or a food treat. Gradually you can lengthen the time between delivery of the reward and the required behaviours.

All your early efforts with training should be working towards channelling self-control in the young dog, so that it learns that patience really is a virtue. By acting in a consistent and relaxed manner in response to the puppy's efforts you will build a framework for calm behaviour.

WHEN THINGS GO WRONG

Dogs are not perfect (just like us). Things don't always go to plan during the course of the day or when training. If this happens occasionally, it really doesn't matter. For example, if, at the

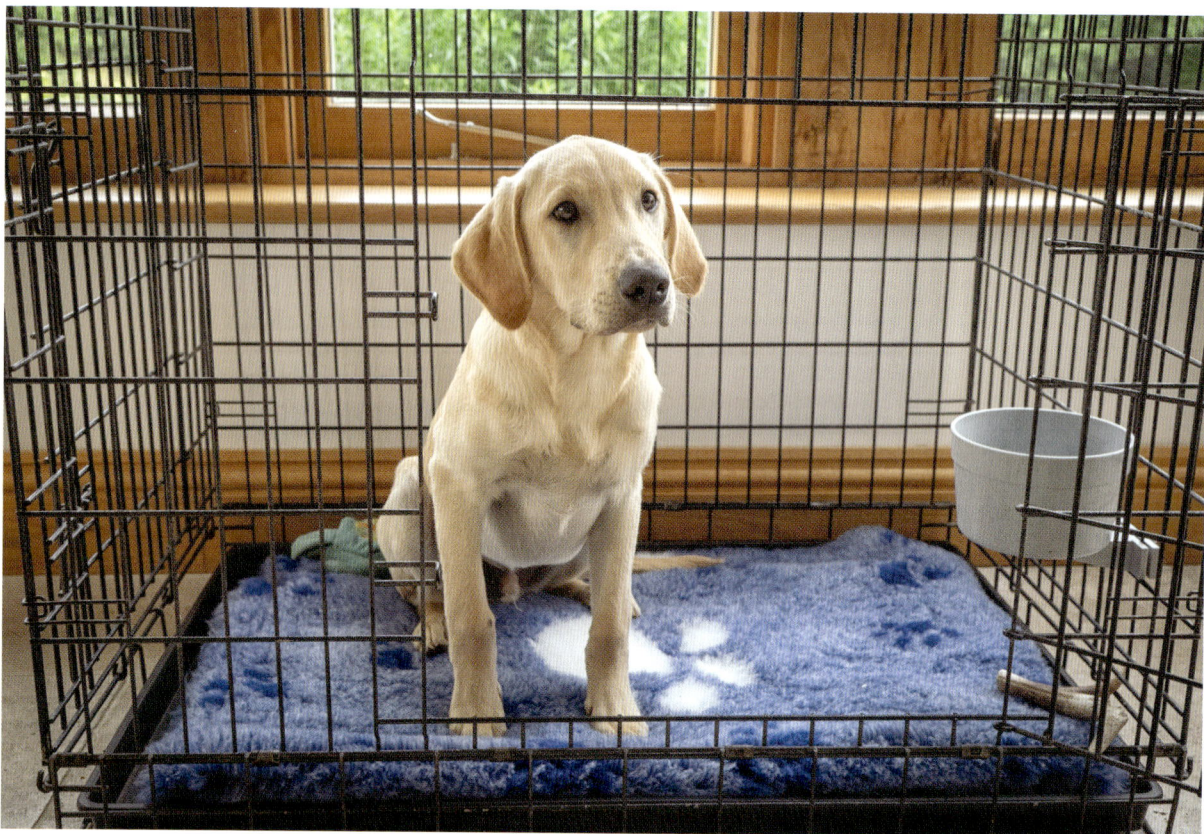

A crate is ideal for night time, or for periods when the puppy cannot be supervised in the house.

age of thirteen weeks, your pup chases a butterfly before coming back to you, or lingers on an interesting scent, this is just 'being a puppy' – its attention span is so limited at that age. However, if it is still doing such things at thirteen months, then that is cause for concern. I remember being mortified on a Christmas day walk when my seven-month-old puppy, Pru, put up and gave chase to a hare! At the time I was convinced that this would be her ruination. Needless to say, we recovered from that minor setback in time. She was ill prepared for that hare (as was I). In later years, that area of her training was complete and I could rely on her completely not to give chase.

Mistakes are not the end of the world: they are inevitable in any training journey. When things go wrong, or the dog doesn't act as you expect it should, it is usually not the dog being evil and plotting to overthrow you, but just that you have not prepared it for the job you have asked of it.

You are trying to get it to do something of which it is not yet capable. This means you need to simplify and retrace some steps in order to refocus on building the good habit that you want.

ENCOURAGING HOLD AND RELEASE

One of the very important elements of foundation training that is easy to work on while the pup is in the house is its attitude to carrying, fetching and eventually delivering to hand all manner of items – some desired and some not! When the pup is playing freely around the home, it will inevitably pick things up from the floor or low surfaces. These items can range from socks, shoes, toys, magazines and doorstops through to more precious items such as the television remote control, a mobile phone, reading glasses or a book.

Whatever the item, I always praise a pup for

Try not to snatch precious items away from the puppy when he takes them, but instead reward him for holding them and replace it with something else he can hold.

carrying something and proudly bringing it to me. I put my hands on the pup's body and stroke it enthusiastically, without making any attempt to take the item away. I praise it and tell it how clever it is. I then take the item carefully from the pup with my chosen release command 'dead', look at the proffered gift, then give it back to the pup again using the word 'hold', and repeat the praise and touch routine.

I want the pup to understand that it is really rewarding for it to hold something in its mouth, and that I am very pleased with it. I will not try and take the article away immediately. I then repeat this routine. If the item is precious – such as a mobile phone or the television remote control – on the second release command I will replace it with something safer and less valuable for the pup to hold, such as a toy or a rolled sock. I never lunge for the item the pup is carrying, or say 'no!', despite what I might be feeling about its safety or the item in its mouth.

In this way, the really young puppy is praised for just carrying, and then releasing and retaking the item. This encourages a very natural hold, without the puppy wanting to drop the item or spit it out. And it means that the puppy is always happy to return to me to show me the 'retrieve', rather than running off and hiding with it, or engaging in 'keep away', or playing with it.

While the pup is in the teething stage, I stop doing any retrieves, and only use soft articles for the puppy to pick up and hold, so as not to cause any mouth discomfort, which I don't want associated with retrieving. Once teething has finished, and a natural retrieve has been established (see

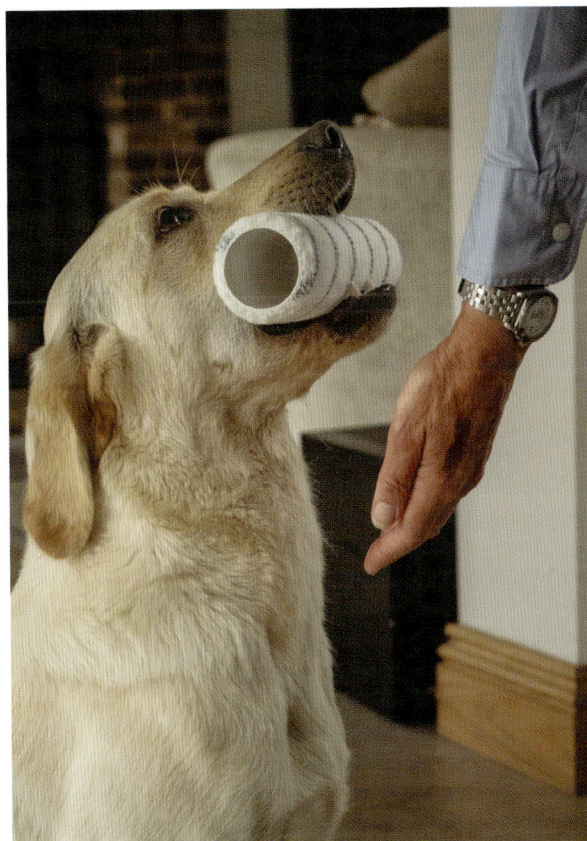

Using a paint roller (new) to teach the concept of 'hold' and 'dead'.

Chapter 8), I return to reviewing the process of holding and releasing on command, and make the whole thing more polished. This becomes my final delivery of the retrieve. The age range when you might think about doing this will vary, but for my own dogs it is usually around eight months old, when I want delivery to be more formal. Up until that point, I accept the puppy just returning to my vicinity quickly, and I am not too concerned with how he presents himself or the dummy. Strength of return is more important at this stage than the actual delivery of the retrieve.

STRETCHING THE ADOLESCENT MIND

The first gundog training book that I ever read was by the late Susan Scales (1992), *Retriever Training*. It may now be considered somewhat 'old-fashioned' in its approach, but the concept she used to form the framework of her book is still relevant. She related the training of a puppy to children's school stages – nursery, primary, secondary, sixth form. This gives the handler a way of ensuring that their training is age (or, more importantly, 'stage') appropriate. It is a mistake to over-face very young dogs with complicated tasks, for which they are not adequately prepared. You wouldn't ask your pre-school child to take an A-level exam. But equally, it is important to ensure that the more intelligent 'graduates' are stretched and challenged when their brains are capable, so they do not become stale or over self-reliant. Think of this as 'streaming' them towards higher level work.

With a young dog, knowing when to hold back and take things slowly, and when to push on, is a skill that you will develop as a trainer over time, as more dogs pass through your hands. Bright young dogs will thrive on a challenge and rise to it. They will naturally 'up their game' when stimulated with novelty. It is a mistake to repeatedly make tasks too easy for this sort of dog. So, training should contain enough of a stretch, without pushing the young dog to a failure.

I have a training colleague and friend who always turns out an extremely fast and confident dog, whilst mine are always more mannered or considered in their work, although

TEN GOLDEN RULES FOR PUPPY TRAINING

1	Build the bond and relationship
2	Set 'house rules'
3	Early conditioning pays dividends
4	Ensure frustration tolerance
5	Practise success
6	Don't dwell on mistakes
7	Train little and often
8	Use a single command only
9	Nurture the desire to carry and hold
10	Train to 'stage' rather than 'age'

they still retain their drive. We often joke that if we swapped puppies for a couple of weeks, we would have the perfect two dogs between us! There is obviously something that he does in his early training that brings out this speed and confidence in his dogs. We've discussed the differences, and it comes down to the work that each of us is giving our young dogs. He tends to do a lot of basic or repetitive exercises where the pup 'knows the drill', and this promotes raw speed and confidence, and a good deal of self-belief. This is a good thing, in that you want a young dog to run out strongly, but it also needs to be done with caution.

I, on the other hand, if I see that a pup is picking things up quickly and has the intelligence to take on board more training, will start to stretch its mind a bit, so that it is having to think more. This means my pup will take guidance from me, looking towards me more, rather than relying on itself or its learned routines. Increasing the challenge within a training exercise will mean less raw, hard-driving pace, but more consideration as the dog is using its brain to try and 'stay with you' and work out what is required.

It is important to read the young dog in front of you, and to continue to give it work that is appropriate to its developing needs. Sometimes this will mean taking a step back, when the youngster is struggling or has been overwhelmed by a new concept, and at other times it will mean pressing on more quickly to stretch the pup a little, and provide extra fodder for its growing brain.

6 AT HEEL

It's very difficult to find a detailed definition or an origin of 'heelwork' on preliminary searches of the internet. *The Oxford English Dictionary* merely describes it as 'the action or practice of walking with one's dog close to one's heel', and gives its origin as mid-nineteenth century. Collins dictionary terms 'at heel' as being '(of a dog) close to and slightly behind its owner'.

In retriever parlance, we largely understand heelwork to be our dog walking close to our left leg, in a consistent and calm position, with its head roughly level with the handler's knee. On the other hand, in competitive obedience classes the Kennel Club regulations state that 'the dog's shoulder should be approximately level with, and reasonably close to, the handler's leg at all times when the handler is walking' (KC Obedience Show Regulations (G Regs) 2019); there is no such required prescription of position for field trials or working tests. The Kennel Club regulations for field trials merely state that 'unsteadiness at heel' is a major fault (J Regs p.21, 2019), and it is up to judges to decide what constitutes unsteadiness. Actual heel position is left largely down to handler preference, and safety (particularly when carrying a gun and swinging round to shoot). The dog that pulls too far ahead is likely to get under the feet of its handler and be dangerous, causing a trip hazard. One that lags too far behind will be unable to mark the fall of birds in front in a walked-up shooting situation.

THE IMPORTANCE OF CLOSE PROXIMITY WORK

Heelwork is much more than just the act of getting tidily from A to B. The dog's position at heel, and its relation to its handler, has a major impact on a lot of the other work that

Photo: Neil Rice

follows. For example, your later work on marking and lining will undoubtedly fall down if the dog is not parallel to the direction you are facing, maintaining the heel position, and tracking your movement as you rotate to face marks.

Looking at heelwork, and the dog's position in relation to its handler, would seem to be a very basic and fundamental thing, and hardly the stuff of an advanced training book. But on the contrary, it is how the dog is relating to you at heel that is critical to the success of your advanced work. If you haven't won the mind of the dog, and gained his respect, at this close proximity around you, then your chance of achieving control when the dog is 100 metres away or more is very slim indeed.

I believe that a champion is made up within two feet of me! How that dog relates to me at heel will eventually dictate how we work together in the field. It isn't all about the eye-catching 300-metre retrieves across a valley – although these do always look impressive. It's about knowing the dog is working with me in a strong relationship, with manners and respect, and a complete understanding of the 'rules of the game'.

SIT OR STAND

I am often asked whether it is better to have a dog sitting or standing at heel, in terms of steadiness. The general sentiment from handlers is that the dog will be steadier if it is sitting down. Sometimes I've questioned students as to why they are insisting on a sit at heel, and they say that they feel the dog will be less likely to run in from a seated position, than if it were standing. My response to this is that *steadiness is a state of mind, not a state of limbs*. I've seen dogs run in from a sitting position at heel as many times, if not more, than from a standing position. The physical position of the limbs makes no difference to the dog's steadiness at heel. That comes from their attitude – what is going on in their head – and how they are relating

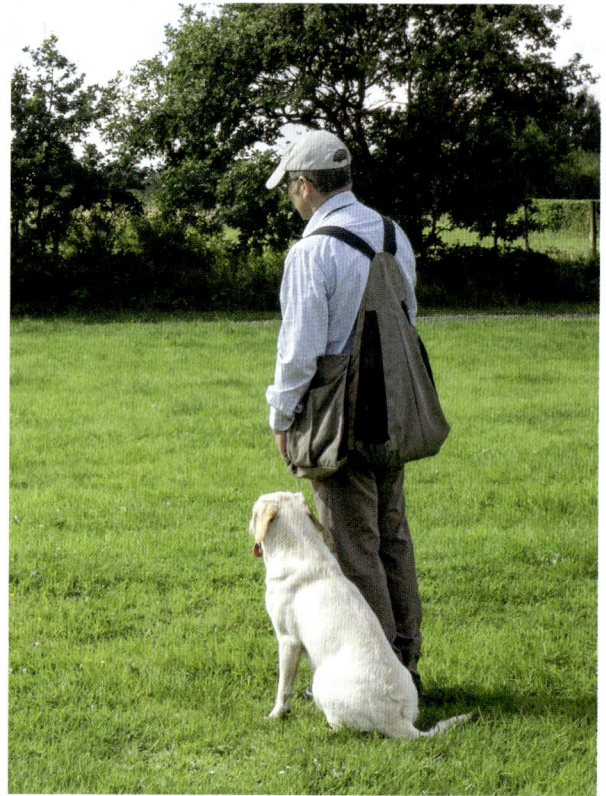

Personal preference dictates whether your dog should stand or sit at heel. In either position, the dog should remain calm and steady by the handler's side.

When walking up, many handlers have their dog standing at heel, whereas when waiting in a drive it is more common to see the dog sitting.

to the stimuli they are receiving.

So, how you position a dog at heel, either sitting or standing, is down to personal preference. I usually have my own dogs standing, as this is natural for them during walked-up shooting (which forms a large proportion of their retrieving work at field trials in the Midlands, East Anglia and further north in the UK), and they can turn quickly with me at heel to mark birds down in front, to the side, or behind the line. But I do also require them to sit when picking up at local shoots or on the peg at a drive. The important point is that the dog maintains the same quiet demeanour and position in relation to heel. You decide on sit or stand, and apply your rules consistently according to context, so that the dog understands its cues. My own dogs are only sent for a retrieve from a standing position, so that forms part of their cue chain to retrieve.

THE 'LURE' METHOD

Most gundog training books will teach you to start your puppy with heelwork on the lead, using the rope slip lead to hold the puppy in the desired position, and checking it if it goes out of position. Once the puppy gets used to this routine on the lead, you then gradually slip the lead off, or wrap it around the puppy's neck so that it still believes that it is attached. I take the reverse approach, in that I teach my puppy the desired heel position off the lead, before I think about introducing it to the lead. This is all done with food treats – small titbits of cocktail sausage, cheese, freeze-dried meat or liver. Anything very tasty will do. I start with pups when they are around twelve weeks old – at this age they have had a chance to bond with you well, and have grown physically so they are big enough for

Use a treat in your left hand to lure the desired heel position, and only deliver the treat when the pup is in the correct position. The left hand will eventually become a target for the puppy.

you to be able to bend down and deliver a treat whilst walking.

To try this method, put the pup on the lawn and then put the treat in front of their nose, using your left hand, and use it to lure them around to your left side to the desired position, where you can let them lick and nibble at the treat just on the side of your leg at knee level. Make a few steps in this manner with their nose pressing against the treat trying to get it, and praise the pup and deliver the treat with that left hand all the while they are making contact with your leg. In this way, the pup begins to understand that this particular position is very rewarding, and they will want to maintain it. If the pup is holding the position, allow it to lick and nibble at the treat, all the while praising it. Using this 'lure' method is a lazier way to achieve a good heel position, compared to clicker training. But I find it works very well, quickly, and is easier to

manage than trying to juggle both a clicker and treat delivery with the correct hand.

If the pup goes to move away because it is distracted by something else, let it go and investigate, then gently lure it back again using the treat in the left hand once more. Reserve any praise until the time that the pup is in the required position, and at that point again praise and deliver the treat. You should only do a couple of repetitions of this game, and should aim to stop before the puppy gets bored. It is something that you can easily do with a puppy indoors too, and fit it around other household activities in the morning or evening. Just a few minutes here and there is enough. You don't want to become boring. All you are trying to do is make the association that being at the 'heel' position, at the left side of your leg, is extremely rewarding, enjoyable and worthwhile.

Only when the pup is achieving this reliably should you start to back-chain the 'heel' command on to it. You don't want to use the cue word until you are entirely confident that the puppy understands the correct position completely and is consistent in it.

By not using a lead, you have not been tempted to maintain the pup in position using resistance. And the puppy in turn has not learned to pull against the lead, as it has never been part of the routine. The puppy has chosen to maintain its position, rather than being forced to hold a position. When you do eventually slip a lead on for the first time, the puppy is already nicely at heel, so the lead will just dangle loosely and not figure as being something to be pulled against. The pup will hold position regardless of the lead being on or off, because it has learnt that this behaviour is highly rewarding.

In addition, if the dog is not in the right position, by not using any form of 'correction' you are not creating any negative associations with heelwork. The dog actively tries to put itself into the position where it knows it will be rewarded.

As the puppy gets older, make your heelwork sessions short and fun (no longer than a minute or two), by incorporating plenty of changes of direction and pace, so that the pup is actively engaging and working to keep up with you. You want him to be 'with you' both in his body position and in his mind.

Later on, when the pup is fully grown, you can revisit this method to 'tidy up' heelwork, so that the youngster is maintaining a completely parallel position to your leg when at heel, both when seated and when turning or standing. Reward the dog when it is in the precise position that you want, and use a non-reward marker, such as 'no' or 'try again', when it is slightly out of position – such as sitting leaning inwards (common when you use food treats to reward, as the dog will start to try to get nearer to the food source), or with its back end drifting out. Encourage the dog to have another go at getting the position perfect, or use the food treat to lure it again into the desired position.

This attention to detail is not just 'window dressing', but will ensure that your dog's footwork is accurate so that it can turn quickly and mark the fall of a bird, and it has its body in the correct position to be sent directly, rather than being wrongly angled for the retrieve. Focusing on the dog's body alignment at heel in this way will mean that the dog is more responsive to your movements, and will also make lining and sending for blinds much more precise.

'PUSH' AND 'PULL' TURNS AT HEEL

Practise turning at heel in the stationary position as well as when walking. This static work will really highlight any inaccuracies in your dog's positioning next to you. Try 90-degree turns to your right, which will mean you are drawing the dog around towards you (pull). This is easy for the dog, as it is rotating freely and maintaining its position next to you, filling the space that you have left for it. Then try 90-degree turns to the left. This is more difficult for the dog as it has to pivot on its hindquarters as you 'push' into its space.

Look at the dog after these turns and notice its body position in relation to you. It should still have its body in alignment with you, from its nose through to the base of its tail. The push and pull are not done physically by touching the dog, but they occur through the dog understanding the concept of 'heel' and through its sense of personal space.

This static turn work can be linked into a clock-face drill of sending the dog for the dummy that it is facing, if it is accurately positioned. The retrieve will reward the dog's correct alignment.

If heelwork is taught in this way, the dog always takes your left leg as its point of reference for being in the correct position. Wherever that left leg goes, the dog should follow and make an effort to track it accurately and maintain his position through that movement. You can test this by standing still but just stepping forwards with your left leg. Your dog should move forwards to stay aligned with this leg, and then move back again when you bring your leg back. Next try stepping back with just the left leg. Again, the dog should move backwards to stay in contact at heel, rather than staying stationary. Conversely, if you step forwards with just the right leg, the dog should maintain its static position at heel in

(a) The dog should maintain its heel position in reference to your left leg. (b) Stepping forwards with the left leg, the dog will move forwards. (c) Stepping forwards with the right leg, the dog will remain in position next to the left leg.

proximity to your left leg, which hasn't moved.

As an added refinement, you can work on the dog always heeling away with you when you strike off with the left leg, and always remaining in a stay when you strike off with the right leg. This is something that is used in competitive obedience, and I have found it useful in early puppy schooling, and later on for walk-ups, as the dog must continue walking with you without a verbal command.

MULTIPLE DOGS

With several dogs, it isn't possible for them all to be at 'heel' in the correct position. Instead, use an alternative command for them to stay in close proximity to you.

If you have more than one dog walking with you, it is impossible for them all to maintain the correct heel position, as only one can be directly next to your leg. Rather than using your heel command for walking several dogs in this manner, it is better to use a separate cue word for this activity. For example, I use 'close', which means that my pack of dogs must all walk with me, gathered around me, either to the right or left, and stay with me – but it's a loose position or grouping, rather than the very specific one of 'heel'. Using this separate cue word means that you don't weaken your 'heel' command, which is reserved for a very specific position.

ATTITUDE

In addition to being critical about the dog's physical position at heel, it is important to note its demeanour, and how it is relating mentally to being at heel and coping with the distractions around it. Ideally you want the dog to be calm and relaxed, but engaged with you, working to keep up with you. It should be marking the fall of retrieves, and be aware of other dogs retrieving, but it should not become overly aroused by this retrieve work.

The dog that is pulling forwards on marks during a walk-up is already 'lost in the head' and not giving primary importance to its handler. Equally, the one that is lagging behind, not concentrating on either the work that is about to happen or its handler, is of similar concern.

This dog has pulled forwards at heel in the excitement of the walk-up. It is more focused on the potential retrieves than holding its position in relation to the handler.

Some dogs become 'pushy' at heel, paddling their feet, lurching forwards, or rising up from a seated position so that they are hovering, poised for action (I call this pneumatic bottom!), in anticipation of being sent to retrieve. All of these things should be noted as being undesirable, and not fulfilling the criteria of 'steady at heel', and the handler should take care not to inadvertently reward this behaviour by sending the dog for retrieves while it is in this over-aroused state. Rather, take time to notice the dog's attitude, and give it feedback as to what you like and don't like.

Although maintaining a good position in relation to his handler, this dog is hovering in anticipation of the retrieve, rather than conducting himself calmly.

Do not send the dog to retrieve until it is settled and calm. This may mean that you spend the majority of a group walk-up session just paying attention to heelwork, and not accepting the retrieves that are offered to you until your dog settles down. Only then can you praise it for calm, relaxed behaviour and send it for the retrieve.

Having to worry about poor heelwork will also impact on your own ability to concentrate on marking and what is happening all around you. It is a distraction that you can do without, particularly in competition, when you need to be alert to the fall of birds to give yourself the best opportunity of picking retrieves efficiently. So it is important to remedy the situation sooner rather than later. And this may mean going back to the beginning again, and re-teaching heelwork from the start, in the manner described, so that the dog truly understands the concept.

When things do go wrong, and the dog does pull out of position, particularly in an environment with a high level of distractions, try not to respond in anger or frustration by using the heel command in a cross voice. Remember that 'heel' is a command, not a correction, and the last thing you want to do is to create confusion by shouting 'heel' when the dog is in the wrong position, or creating a negative association for the command. Instead, use a vocal correction, such as 'no' or 'ah, ah', and then when the dog does make an effort to put himself back into the right position, mark this with praise and a reward.

SENDAWAY POSITION

When does heel, and its meaning of the specific position of the dog in relation to a handler's left leg, not mean heel? The answer to this conundrum for some handlers appears to be when they are about to send the dog for a retrieve. They have gone through all the basics, and taught the young dog the required position at heel, both walking up and in a static position. Then they go to send their dog on a directed retrieve (memory mark or blind, where they have to give the dog a line), and all thought of the dog maintaining this position at heel is forgotten. Some handlers step back with their left leg, almost stepping

This handler has stepped back with the left leg, allowing the dog to be off heel (in front of the left leg) before sending it.

behind the dog, before pointing with their right hand to the direction of the retrieve. And they don't expect the dog to follow their left leg at this point to maintain heel position. Others allow their dogs to pull so far forwards in the sendaway, in anticipation of the retrieve, that the handler is practically 'sending the tail'. In either case, the previous good heel position seems to have temporarily vanished.

How does a dog reconcile this? In both cases, heel would appear to mean 'remain in place next to the handler's left leg, unless you are going to be sent for a retrieve,

and then it is acceptable to move out of the heel position or to pull forwards'.

Two issues arise from this. The first is that the dog learns that pulling forwards is the 'go position', and therefore it is positively reinforcing to pull forwards – to achieve the retrieve. This is then likely to transfer to heelwork in general, whereby the dog starts pulling forwards as you are walking up (to better mark the birds) in anticipation of the retrieves to follow. By allowing the dog to pull forwards in the sendaway position you are being inconsistent in your definition of 'heel', and permitting the dog to interpret it in a

The dog has pulled forwards in the sendaway, resulting in the handler being behind the dog to send it. Notice that the arm lining the dog is mostly behind the dog's field of vision.

Correct heel position at sendaway, with the dog standing calmly and maintaining its position in relation to the handler's left leg.

variety of ways.

Secondly, with the dog so far in front of the handler, it doesn't have much to go on in terms of taking a good line to the retrieve. The dog does not have the benefit of the handler's full arm to indicate the direction of travel. This can become problematic for the handler, when a higher degree of accuracy of lining is required for advanced retrieve work on blinds.

Pay critical attention to the dog's position at heel, not only whilst walking up and in static work, but also in how it is relating to heel when it is being sent to retrieve. It should remain consistent in attitude and position. I am clear with my own dogs that there is never a time when heel does not mean heel. That sets an easy framework for them to understand.

7 PLANNING AND MANAGING TRAINING

Luck is what happens when preparation meets opportunity.

Attributed to the Roman philosopher, Seneca

Once you have moved beyond the puppy bonding, play and initial foundation stage, you will need to adopt a more structured approach to your training. Thinking about an overall strategy, and planning your sessions to meet your goals, will yield better results than haphazard training sessions. Planning provides a structure for us to follow, and helps us to keep the end goal in sight. Effective planning is key to success in many areas of life, and gundog training is no different.

Train with your end goal in mind – whether that is winning a field trial, picking up, or having a polished peg dog. Each of these roles is subtly different (although it is possible eventually to do all three with the same dog). It is important to understand what you are aiming for, so that you tailor the focus of your training accordingly.

Think about your priorities. This will help keep you on track and heading in the right direction. Because it's a hobby and a nice pastime, it often seems to me that people enjoy going out to train, but with very little idea of what they are hoping to achieve from the session, and for their overall training. They are enjoying a pleasant afternoon out, and there is nothing wrong with that, but they aren't putting as much thought into the activity as they perhaps should if they want to train more proficiently and professionally. And attending group sessions is sometimes an especially lazy way of training! It doesn't require any forward planning, or thinking about where you are going to put retrieves, why and for what aim. Largely, you just turn up, and let somebody else do the throwing and direct the session. You hand over a lot of the responsibility to the designated trainer. The good ones will take the time to know your dog, and try to tailor their sessions accordingly, but others, with busy large classes, will set up standard exercises, where you just attend and run your dog through their set-ups.

Those that have a clear idea of where they are going and plan effectively will

Good trainers will tailor their group classes to the needs of the individual handlers and their dogs.

CASE STUDY: USING A SPREADSHEET TO RECORD TRAINING DATA

Subject: Pru, six-month-old Labrador puppy.

Objective: To teach the foundation basic obedience behaviours, and ensure that they were conditioned in a variety of locations with various distractions.

Action: I recorded all the obedience behaviours that I thought would be useful on to a dated weekly spreadsheet, and logged each time I had trained one of the elements each day. I also noted what training ground I had used, and if there had been any distractions.

Result: All Pru's basic obedience work was recorded in a methodical way, and I was able to see at a glance if I had missed out any areas over the weeks. Keeping the spreadsheet enabled me to keep track of how many times I had repeated certain foundation behaviours, and under what level of distraction.

be more successful in achieving their aims. If we look at sports coaches, they set up appropriate programmes for their élite athletes and plan their activities to gain the best results. We should try to do the same for our canine athletes.

DIARIES AND JOURNALS

A training diary or log is a good idea, if you have the discipline to keep one. Making a note of what you have done with your dog in regular sessions or at a certain stage is a useful reminder, and in the following years, with later dogs, it can sometimes be helpful to look back on notes that may shed light on how to deal with similar issues. A log can help you remember the things you have done and how your dog has related to the exercises. It will help you to move on methodically.

Writing things down can help a trainer consider how to achieve an objective or solve a particular problem. It helps to clarify the process, and means that you can plan your time more effectively in the field. Make a note of any areas of weakness that you notice in training, and plan your work to improve them. For instance, if the dog has become too handler reliant on hunting, or isn't focusing on running a line for blinds, single out the particular issue and work on a strategy to improve it.

It is also a good idea to use a journal or a spreadsheet to record issues relating to the health and welfare of your dog, such as regular worming or flea and tick treatments, or for individual illnesses or injuries. In addition, for bitches, keep a note of the dates they had their seasons, and if relevant, what their progesterone readings were prior to breeding.

TIMEFRAMES

Often people will ask 'At what age should I start doing X?' or 'How old is your pup?'. For me, it is more important to ask 'At what stage?' rather than 'At what age?'. Your nine-month-old puppy may be ready to do something that another person's dog is still not doing at eighteen months. Dogs mature at different rates, and handlers have different abilities and differing resources. It is very tempting to compare your dog to another person's, and to try and keep up with fellow handlers, or with littermates. But we have to treat each dog individually and according to its capabilities. Work with the dog in front of you, not to where you think you should be at this point.

My 'training year' tends to start sometime at the end of February. The shooting season is over, and I like my dogs to have a few weeks total break before we resume training again. During that late winter/early spring time I usually go 'back to basics' with my team, and re-visit some of the core skills and obedience work, which is the bedrock of all our more advanced gundog

	MON	TUES	WED	THURS	FRI	SAT	SUN
HEELWORK							
On lead	1	1	1	1	1	1	1
Off lead and whistle sits	1	1	1	1	1	1	1
Figure 8	1						
About turns	1						
Zigzags/weave/circle							
Varied speed	1						
Distractions		Unfamiliar dogs	Hare		Own dogs		Own dogs
Location	Swith wood	Sugar beet	Sugar beet	Swith wood	Baines field	Baines field	Billa Barra
STAYS							
1 min heel stay	1			1			1
Walkaway and return	1			1			
2 min sit	1		1	1			
Clock walk	1						
Dummy thrown	1			1			1
Out of sight	1		1	1			
RECALLS							
Recall from free play	1	1	1	1	1	1	1
Recall from sit	1	1	1	1		1	1
Recall with dummy							
Finish to heel	1			1		1	
Retrieves							
Hold dummy				1			
Short visual retrieve				1			
Memory mark						1	1

An example spreadsheet to record foundation obedience training.

work. I will also review their handling skills. At this time of year, too, pups born the previous spring are also starting to reach the age where they need the most input, and are learning lots.

The length of training sessions should suit the dog. With youngsters, I keep the lessons very short, and prefer to do just five to ten minutes with a puppy. The attention span of a young dog is limited, and the emphasis should be on short bursts of learning that are fun and rewarding.

With the older dogs, their maturity means that sessions can be longer, as their attention span is greater. Having said that, I still prefer to keep my sessions fairly short. When you are working on a one-to-one basis with a single dog, you can actually achieve quite a lot in a short space of time; if you make the session too long, you risk giving the dog too many retrieves, which may lead to staleness. You want to avoid boring the dog with over-training. My mantra has always been 'qual-

Refreshing some basic handling with a young dog.

ity over quantity'. If you plan your sessions properly, you will get more out of them, in a much shorter space of time.

KEEP TRAINING SESSIONS SIMPLE

In addition to keeping sessions relatively short when training alone, try to look at just one or two specific elements that need work. Keeping things simple allows you to focus on quality in each of the behaviours you are looking at. Rather than setting up complex tests for your dogs, separate out individual skills from the total retrieve process. For example, with an older dog you might be looking at maintaining a tight area on hunting, or with a young pup you may go out just to practise casting left or right. Try not to introduce more than one main concept into each of these

training sessions. This is your 'break-down' work.

Then, when you do set up a complete retrieving exercise, try to look at the various elements of it critically and improve on just one at time. For example, if you are focusing on strengthening the outrun to long memory marks and the dog swaps dummies at the point of collection, try to ignore the latter for the time being, but log it to address another time. You don't want to chastise the dog, or communicate displeasure for his swapping, when you are actually overjoyed that he has just powered out 200 yards with confidence and style. So, praise the dog for the strength of his outrun, at the time, so he knows that he has got that bit right. But make a mental note about working on swapping in a separate session at a later date. This is where a training journal is useful, as you can make a note in it here to remind yourself if necessary. By working on each stage of a retrieve individually, you can communicate clearly to the dog what is required, and give precise feedback on its behaviour at the correct time. Once one part is learned, you can move on in manageable steps.

I always try to end my training sessions on a positive note. Sometimes, if a session has gone on for a while and the dog has struggled, it is tempting to keep pushing on to try to achieve what you want to in that single outing. This rarely has a happy ending. Getting cross or frustrated with your tired dog will only have a negative effect on him as well as you. It is usually better to draw a line, and end with something positive that the dog can do well. Try to end with some sort of success. This leaves a positive association, and you can pick up again another day if more work is required on a particular issue.

LEARNING CONSOLIDATION IN DOWN TIME

Often after the dog has had a rest and time to digest, things seem to improve and he may appear to have finally 'got it'. This phenomenon is often referred to as 'latent learning', although that is somewhat of a misnomer – perhaps 'learning consolidation' would be a more accurate description. The feeling is that, sometimes, performance appears to improve after a rest or some 'down time', when things seem to 'gel'. This

A period of rest often helps to consolidate learning.

is why many trainers, including myself, do not advocate training every single day, but actually give their dogs a day off in between sessions, so they can digest their learning. It seems that the brain stores the information in long-term memory and is able to assimilate this learning for use at a later date when required. This rest period contributes to a greater fluency in knowledge. We therefore need to ensure that each training session is rewarding, as it is hard to perform latent learning if the dog is stressed.

Another thing to consider is finishing with a wind-down or 'play time'. A recent interesting study (Affenzeller *et al*, 2016) found that ending a training session with play has a positive effect on learning in dogs. The researchers observed two groups of Labradors that were trained in a particular task.

The first group were given individual training sessions followed by a period of rest, whereas the second group were given the same training but allowed a play session afterwards (walking and then either fetching a ball or playing tug). The researchers concluded that physiological arousal (indicated by raised heart rate and salivary cortisol levels) produced chemical changes in the brain, which influenced memory.

Hormonal responses during arousal in humans is known to have an effect on the hippocampus and amygdala, leading to improvements in memory (Osborne *et al*, 2015). So it seems that a similar phenomenon happens with our dogs. As well as the beneficial effects on the dog's memory, it is likely that a short session of play will give your dog a break after training and strengthen your relationship with him. So, whilst you should treat training sessions seriously, it is worth bearing in mind the proverb that says 'all work and no play makes Jack a dull boy'. Try to strike a balance between work, rest and play.

STAY ONE STEP AHEAD

With young dogs, repetition of key elements builds confidence. Using the same commands and cues for desired behaviours each time is

Play has a beneficial effect on memory, as well as strengthening relationships. (Photo: Patrice Fellows)

important, and building routines helps dogs with their understanding – but we should be careful not to become too regimented. This can lead to the dog becoming bored or stale, and can affect drive. Repetition has its place. But it is pointless just going over and over things once dogs have learnt them. Fully trained dogs don't need lots of repetition. They just need keeping fit, happy and polished. Boring an experienced dog with repetitive retrieves is counterproductive.

Relying too much on routine will lead to a clever dog starting to anticipate commands. So it is up to us to stay one step ahead of this type of dog, and become less predictable to them. When the dog thinks he knows the exercise and goes to pre-empt the handler's command we know that we need to mix things up a bit, so that the dog has to pay more attention to what the handler actually wants.

As your training session progresses, watch the dog carefully for any sign that he is cottoning on to what you might be thinking of doing next. If you see any signs of anticipation, immediately change tack. For example, you may have planned to bring in a dog on a recall with the view to stopping him with the whistle half-way to direct him right-handed to a retrieve. When you call him in, you notice that he isn't putting full power into his recall because he has guessed that he is going to be stopped and redirected. So at this point you need to abandon the exercise on redirection that you had planned, and switch immediately to the full recall back to you. And repeat this again, reinforcing the recall with a reward, to regain the momentum that was lost by the dog predicting what he thought was going to happen next. In this way, the dog is put on the back foot, as he has to rely on, and trust you to gain his next reward.

Try always to stay one step ahead of the dog. If you see signs of him pre-empting your next command, change your approach. You don't want him to think he knows best – you want him to give you his full attention and trust, and for him to be completely receptive to your next command or direction.

Being perceptive in your training will be a huge asset to you. Good trainers have the ability to be

If your dog begins to anticipate your training routine, change your approach so that he doesn't pre-empt your command.

responsive and adaptive. They are flexible enough to alter their routines, changing things to take on board the dog's progress, capability and environmental conditions in the time available.

WORKING IN DIFFERENT TERRAINS

Training a retriever to an advanced level will mean that eventually you have to accustom it to a huge range of situations, including being able to work in a variety of diverse terrains from woodland, arable farmland and root crops, through to open moorland, bracken banks and fell. You will need to give the dog a thorough grounding in different terrains, and exposure

Training 'on location' gives your dog exposure to a wide variety of terrain and experiences.

to the types of 'barrier' that he may encounter there, such as rivers, streams, lakes, ditches, hedges, tree plantations, fences, stone walls and gullies.

With the rise of several purpose-built training venues, and trainers setting themselves up on stunning natural grounds to give group training, we are spoilt for choice when it comes to this sort of 'exposure' training. These grounds, usually used by a large group of trainers, are ideal for putting 'miles on the clock' and giving your dog experience in unfamiliar types of terrain. They will help to stretch the capabilities of your dog as well as testing you as a handler. They are where you will be able to see if your day-to-day training translates to different situations – and they will give you a chance to proof your commands in a variety of settings.

However, they are not where you go to teach your dog basic commands. I remember many years ago taking a young novice dog for a day shooting rabbits in Northumberland. It was our first time out on such an excursion. The scenery and terrain were fantastic, and the experience that it gave the dogs running up and down the line of guns to retrieve the shot rabbits was inval-

uable, and like nothing we had done before. But I soon found out that it wasn't the place to teach a stop whistle! This should have been firmly in place before making such an excursion. So the day gave me and my dog a very valuable grounding in working, and ignoring, shot scent on the ground. And it gave the dog experience of running the line to unseen rabbit retrieves on unfamiliar terrain. But more importantly, it highlighted to me that I need to teach my basics properly at home first.

For me, then, the majority of my training is done 'at home', whether that is in the garden with young pups, in a nearby field, or at a local park or forest ground. It is a 'one-on-one' session where I can cement my basics, ensure they are understood, and gradually generalize them to more distracting environments. In addition to this, I will meet up with friends at local grounds to 'self-help', setting up retrieves for each other, in particular marks, which cannot be done alone or without help. As pleasant as it is to go away 'venue training', and enjoy the challenge of new grounds and surrounds, there is no substitute for ensuring that your background work is thoroughly complete.

Stone walls may be an unfamiliar obstacle for some dogs.

including approaching obstacles from an angle. So you know you have more work to do when you get home.

TEACHING VERSUS TESTING

On a day-to-day basis, my own training is concentrated on teaching rather than testing. With young dogs, I am coaching them in new skills in a low distraction environment (such as the garden or field), and trying to build up the degree of difficulty gradually over time. Once they have grasped the basic concept and are performing it reliably, I will move on to conditioning, or generalizing, the command. This is my 'bread and butter' training for more advanced dogs, still using repetition to build confidence in the skill in varied locations, and varying the set-up incrementally.

My training process is broadly as follows:

- **Teaching** – new skills and commands in low distraction environments
- **Conditioning** – generalizing the concept in new locations or contexts
- **Testing** – setting up a test for the skill in an unfamiliar location to see how well the training has been proofed
- **Reconditioning** – if necessary, adding new elements, degrees of difficulty or distraction into building the skill

TESTING OUR DOGS' ABILITIES

It is on unfamiliar grounds and in new settings that we find our dogs' abilities are really tested. Often in these group situations, complex retrieves are set up for handlers to stretch their dogs. So we move more into the realms of testing our dogs rather than teaching them.

These sorts of 'test' have a value in highlighting areas that require more work, and can be used to inform training back home. For example, you have taught your dog to jump across a ditch at home, and to cross a small brook in a nearby field. But when you get to Northumberland he struggles to negotiate a fence on top of a steep gully on a diagonal angle. He has learnt the basics of jumping, and he is comfortable with crossing obstacles squarely, but he is not accustomed to holding his line on a diagonal across unfamiliar obstacles. This skill has not yet been fully conditioned to apply to absolutely every scenario,

Dogs enjoying some downtime after a day training on the moor.

confidence to know that you have prepared the dog adequately for that situation. So that takes the hope and chance out of the situation, or at least limits it.

If you haven't taught your dog to jump properly, it may be that he has the guts or enough drive on the day for the adrenalin to take him over that obstacle for the retrieve, but more than likely he will stop at the unfamiliar obstacle and see it as a barrier. It isn't his fault, but your own, that he is ill prepared. But how much better are his chances, and your own confidence, if you have prepared him fully by teaching him to jump a variety of obstacles in a range of situations?

To use the phrase widely attributed to Gary Player (1962): 'The harder I practise, the luckier I get.' Although you cannot take all the chance or luck out of many gundog situations – shooting and field trialling are organic, 'natural' sports – you can prepare the dog for a large variety of scenarios over time through methodical training.

METHODICAL TRAINING

If your training is effective, the question of *hoping* for a good outcome shouldn't come into the analysis – unless it's 'I hope this pup will become my next Field Trial Champion'! For example, if you reach a competition and see a fence included in one of the working tests, you shouldn't *hope* your dog will go over it. If your training has been thorough, you will have the

8 NATURAL ABILITY

Good marking is essential in a retrieving dog as it should not disturb ground unnecessarily. Judges should give full credit to a dog which goes straight to the fall and gets on with the job. Similarly, the ability to take the line of a hare, wounded rabbit or bird should be credited.

J(A)4f, UK Kennel Club Field Trial Regulations

With marking being so important to the role of a retriever, it is surprising that, on the whole, in the UK, we don't dedicate more structured time to this important aspect of gundog work. But most of the training books available spend little more than a cursory few paragraphs discussing this fundamental part of retriever work. If you go rough shooting, or take part in walked-up field trials, the majority of retrieves will be seen or markable. Being able to mark accurately and efficiently will, therefore, give your dog the competitive edge in these situations, over those that have to be handled to the fall.

My observation is that dogs in mainland Europe are often better markers, not because of any particular inherited ability but due to the way they have been taught and trained. Furthermore in these countries there are also usually much lower densities of game on the ground, and in some countries there is no gundog work on live game at all, so handlers will often allow their dogs to range further and work without handler input to produce the retrieve. In the UK, we are much more conscious about disturbing ground where live game might be. In this respect, the dogs in mainland Europe come to rely more upon themselves and their own natural game-finding abilities, than from the control of their handlers. With less input offered, or available, from handlers, it is possible that these dogs have taught themselves to become more effective markers.

You will often hear people say that their dog is a 'superb marking dog' or a 'natural marker', and it does seem that some dogs have more natural aptitude or desire than others. But largely, marking is an acquired or trained skill, just like the others that we teach our dogs.

Seeing and running towards injured prey is part of the chase or hunt instinct in gundogs – this is known as 'prey drive'. It is a natural behavior, and is not something that you should have to teach a well-bred gundog to do. Ideally the retriever will run a direct line efficiently to the area of the fall. However, by working through a systematic process and practising appropriately, the trainer is able to fine tune this innate behaviour, helping the retriever to judge depth and line more accurately and hone its perception when it comes to marking in challenging terrains and conditions.

It may be the popularity of working tests, and to some extent picking up, that has led to a different emphasis in UK gundog training towards refining control work over marking. Other than sending a dog for runners during the drive, most of a picking-up dog's retrieves will be blinds, or very delayed marks. And for working-test dogs, quite often, once the dog has worked its way through the ranks of Novice and into Open test competition, the main focus tends to be on longer or more complex blinds, where the dog has to rely on the handler to direct it to the area to hunt. In Open level working tests, marks are often delayed, to be taken only after the blind retrieve is completed, so they can be tackled similarly to blind retrieves.

But if we train our dogs to become better markers, then there is less need for handler input and control. There is nothing better than watching a dog 'gear down' as it reaches the expected area of fall, and work the area to find the bird using its own natural ability. Dogs that believe the information from their eyes will get to the area promptly and hold the ground, switching to their nose to locate the bird or dummy once they are there.

TEACHING A DOG TO MARK

The process of teaching a dog to mark can begin in early puppyhood, before any concept of steadiness. Gently restrain your young puppy in your arms. Get his attention with a bit of mock pheasant noise and throw his toy or a ball on to the carpet, if you are working indoors, or on to a mown lawn if you are outside. You are looking for him to watch the object, and as it hits the ground, release him immediately (and use a vocal command only), before he tries to struggle free or averts his gaze. With a very young puppy, you will only do this a couple of times, so as not to bore him.

Gradually you will start to insist that his body remains still and calm before you send him. If he tries to struggle free before you release him, then you simply walk out to the toy with him and pick it up. This process can be transferred to an adolescent dog that is unsteady by holding him on a short tag or handle collar while he watches the dummy thrown, and releasing him when he is 'locked on' to it. Ensure that the dog is orientated squarely towards the mark, so that it can run directly towards it with its body and head in alignment. This is important so that the dog is taking a 'snapshot' of the fall, facing it directly.

At first you will send the dog straightaway, so that it learns that if it stares at the retrieve and doesn't take its eyes off it, it is sent. Then you will lengthen the time between the dummy hitting the ground and the sendaway command, so that the dog has to remain steady before being sent. The cues for the dog to learn that it will be sent to retrieve are: watch the object; stay locked on to it; remain quiet, calm and still; then the vocal command to retrieve (usually the dog's name). If the dog takes his eyes off the dummy before being sent, the handler simply walks out and picks up the dummy, and restarts the exercise. The dog then starts to see a pattern. Remaining

Gently restrain the pup while you throw the retrieve, and when he is 'locked on' to it, release him.

locked on he is sent, but if he looks away he isn't sent.

As you progress, vary the time you wait before sending the dog for the mark – sometimes sending immediately and at other times waiting for longer – so that you are confident that the dog is acting consistently and not just waiting for a set time to elapse before being sent.

The above introduction to marking is done on your own, throwing the dummy yourself, so that there is no other distraction out in the field where the dog is looking. You should also use a bright white or contrast dummy that the dog can see clearly when it is on the ground.

INITIALLY THROW A SINGLE DUMMY
When teaching your dog to mark, always throw a single dummy only. This is how the dog will learn to mark and lock on. Eventually you can move on to double marks, but in terms of the retrieves that this will give the dog, you are actually then performing a straight mark and a memory mark, or two memory marks depending on the order in which the two retrieves are taken.

Throwing doubles, then, means you are adding memory into the equation as well as just marking. When the retrieves go wrong, in this case, it

With a young dog you can use a 'tag' collar to hold him in the correct position while he marks the dummy.

The retrieve needs to be clearly visible for the dog to be able to mark it accurately.

is sometimes hard to know whether this was due to poor marking in the first place, or just poor memory. So while the dog is learning the art of successful marking, keep things simple and only use single marks.

USE HIGHLY VISIBLE DUMMIES

When practising marks, it is essential to use dummies that are visible to the dog, either white dummies or two-tone contrast dummies. If the dog can't pick out the dummy, then it isn't a mark. Also, think about the background: is there dark woodland behind where the mark is being thrown, or a hill, which means the dummy doesn't break the skyline for the dog to see clearly? Poor light and landscape features can make marking

conditions more difficult.

Another thing to consider is whether the retrieve is markable from the height of the dog, and not just from the handler's height. If you crouch down next to your dog, you may be surprised to see what things look like from this angle: it is quite enlightening. The smallest of variations in height of terrain or cover can make a big difference to what the dog sees.

THE SOLO TRAINER

Necessarily a lot of gundog training is done on your own, but it is hard to give your dog very long marks, as you will be limited to the distance that you can throw with the dog at your side. And dogs often learn the distance that their handlers can throw. Having said that, by using the method described above, you can teach your dog to mark very accurately, as you are giving him the techniques for success. This will readily translate to longer distance marks, or marks into more complicated terrain.

Remote-controlled automated launchers can be of use for stretching distance on marks, but the use of these comes with a word of caution. Often dogs will run towards the point where they hear the 'bang' come from, or towards the unit itself because they can see it. Once they get near to it, they will then pick up the trail of cordite from the hollow inside of the launcher dummy and will follow it to locate the retrieve. Dogs can learn this pattern and rely on scent to guide them to the dummy, so you can't be sure that they are actually marking accurately.

Solo trainers can also go out and throw marks for their dog and return to its side. But these will be delayed marks, with the added distraction of the dog watching you walk all the way there and back.

As your training progresses, if you have the help of a dummy thrower this can be a huge benefit. And it is for this reason that many people attend group sessions or travel to different trainers, so they can work on marks at distance with their dog.

WHEN THINGS GO WRONG

When practising marks and when the dog has not made a good job of getting directly to the fall, you have a number of options, depending on the type of dog and his level of experience.

With a young dog that has nearly got there but is just struggling to locate the dummy, you can go out and help him, and encourage him to remain in the area. Use praise, and try to keep him at his job to find it. This will reassure him that he was correct in his mark, and that he just needs to work harder to find the dummy with his nose. Once he has located the dummy, it would be worth resetting this exercise but in an area with less difficult (lower) cover, to reinforce his confidence in marking and judging distance, before returning to the same area of more challenging cover.

If the dog goes really out of the area on his mark, powers straight through the area with no attempt to slow down, or doesn't reach the area at all, pick up the dummy, call him back and reset the whole scenario again. There is no point in persevering and letting the dog eventually find the dummy by meritless effort alone, as the dog has already proved that it didn't mark accurately.

If your dog is doing a good job, but has just short marked (common with younger dogs) or over-shot (common with older dogs), try leaving him alone to see if he can self-correct. The dog has a reasonable idea of the line and the depth he should run to, but perhaps because of ground factors (undulating ground or difficult cover) or due to restricted vision, he has just got the distance slightly wrong. He is convinced that this is where the dummy should be, so stops and hunts there. In this situation, it is best to wait and see if, after an efficient search in the area, he will then try searching either further back or further forwards, knowing that he has his line right.

If you can allow a dog to do this in training, it provides an excellent learning tool for him, and it also means that he will have the ability to self-correct if necessary when you are in competition. For example, if your dog is working out of sight in cover and marks short, he will be more likely to adjust his distance if he is not successful straightaway, rather than moving off completely, or stopping and waiting to be handled.

Of course, there is a danger that if you never step in and handle your dog on a mark, he will become used to not being handled on marks. So periodically you should pick opportunities to handle the dog when he hasn't found on his own. Usually downwind marks provide an ideal opportunity for this. Once the dog has gone well beyond winding distance, you can safely step in and handle, to ensure that he is still receptive to being handled, when necessary, on marks.

Overall, though, when working on marks, it is preferable to call the dog back and set it up again, keeping the exercise the same and not changing it. With marked retrieves, you are looking for the dog's natural ability, not control. Obviously in a test or trial situation you will need to handle if the dog is not picking the mark accurately without intervention. But this is damage limitation, and if you train the dog to mark well, these instances where handler intervention is needed will become fewer and fewer.

USING THE WIND

It is extremely important to know in which direction the wind is blowing when you are practising marks, and to use it to your advantage in training. If you have a young dog, throwing a retrieve so that he has to run into the wind can help draw your dog out that bit of extra distance as

Marked retrieves are a test of the dog's natural ability, rather than the handler's control. (Photo: Sue Worrall)

he picks up the scent cone as he nears the mark. With more experienced dogs, downwind marks will really test your dog's marking accuracy, as he will not be able to rely on his nose, unless he runs past the dummy. You want to see the dog start sensibly, slowing into the area, and then switching to using its nose to locate the dummy.

In a cross-wind, a dog may run past the dummy upwind of it by just a few centimetres and fail to catch its scent. Whereas conversely, it may miss the mark on the downwind side by several metres, but wind it from a long distance away. Also, running marks with a cross-wind will help you to teach your dog to hold his line in uncomfortable conditions, without sinking the wind.

Be aware of the role that the wind plays when you set up your marks. And be prepared, in some instances, to let the wind do the work when your dog reaches the right area in relation to the retrieve.

MEMORY MARKS

Dogs have the potential to remember more than one mark, and their memory, like our own, can be improved with practice. The way animals (and humans) remember the location of objects once they are out of sight is through 'object permanence' – that is, knowledge that the object is still there even if it is no longer visible. For example, when a shot bird falls into cover, it still exists.

Dogs have been tested to demonstrate that they have an understanding of object permanence, although it is not as developed as that in humans, primates and some corvids. A study carried out by Miller *et al* (2009) observed that there were three things that prevented dogs from finding hidden objects. These were first, a significant time delay; second, changing the position of the dog in relation to the hidden object; and third, interference by a human. Some dogs coped better or worse with these interrupters.

We can immediately relate these three things that make object permanence more difficult to dogs in the shooting field, and how their marking ability would be affected. For example, the first would represent a delayed mark, where time had elapsed before the dog was sent for the retrieve. The second would be where the dog had been taken away from its initial position where it had marked the retrieve, and then been sent for it from somewhere else; and the third would be distractions from the handler or other people, either talking or indicating other birds that had been seen. All these scenarios would affect how

SAVED BY ITS NOSE!

I once watched a 'run off' of two dogs for first place in a working test. They were set a long downwind mark in some low cover. The first dog ran towards the area of the fall at a strong pace, then as she got about a foot or two short, put her nose down and started hunting the area, successfully picked, and returned with pace. The second dog ran the same way but a bit faster, and travelled quickly through the area of the fall. He sped past the dummy, but his head snapped round as he winded it, and he then retraced his steps to the retrieve. The murmur from the gallery was 'Wow, that was a great mark!'.

The judges put their heads together, and all rightly concurred that the first dog was in fact the better marking dog. It had accurately judged the area of the fall and found there. Although the second dog looked flashy, if it had not been 'right for wind' then it would still have been travelling in a straight line for some distance further. It didn't have an accurate concept of where the retrieve lay.

The good marking dog regulates its speed as it reaches a downwind mark, understanding that it has reached the area of the fall, rather than powering out on a straight line and relying on its nose to 'save' it as it sails straight through and past the area.

you sent your dog for a retrieve, and whether you still treated it as a marked retrieve, or whether it had become a blind retrieve for the dog.

When practising memory marks, vary the length of time before you send the dog, as well as the type of retrieve article. For example, if you have a very delayed mark, try using a large or very visual dummy so that the dog will quickly be successful if it goes to the correct area, rather than having a long struggle to find the retrieve. For memory marks that are more recent, try using a smaller retrieve article, such as a tennis ball, to extend the dog's commitment to hunting the area while he is still confident in his memory of the mark.

MARKING DRILLS

When you have the use of a dummy thrower, it is worth practising marks. But think about the thrower (and shot, if used) in relation to the thrown dummy, as well as in relation to the wind. Quite often the dummy thrower positions himself at a reasonable distance from the handler and their dog, and throws the dummy squarely out to their side at a perpendicular angle. After a while the dog will learn this pattern, in that if they run out to the distance of the thrower and

the shot, they will find the dummy in the vicinity, either directly to the right or left. With these squared-off or 'flat' marks, it is then very difficult to tell if the dog is judging the mark well, or just running to the sound of the shot or the thrower.

To accustom the dog to judging marks more accurately, it is better to ask your thrower to throw either angled back or angled forward marks. In this way, the dog will have to adjust its distance in relation to the thrown dummy, rather than just the thrower.

As well as angled marks, also work on varying the distance of the retrieves. With advanced dogs, it is very tempting always to work on longer and longer retrieves, rather than simpler, short retrieves. But this is a mistake, as you need to be able to pick both. Those who compete in field trials may be familiar with the statement: 'There's no point training for the run-off if you can't make it through the first round.' Typically, in the first round of a retriever stake the retrieves will be relatively short, and taken from the guns nearest to the handlers and dogs. Later on, retrieves are stretched so that the dog is working at greater distances, often down the line. And in a run-off, the dogs may be stretched again in terms of distance and dif-

Having somebody else to throw dummies for you is vital for practising marks.

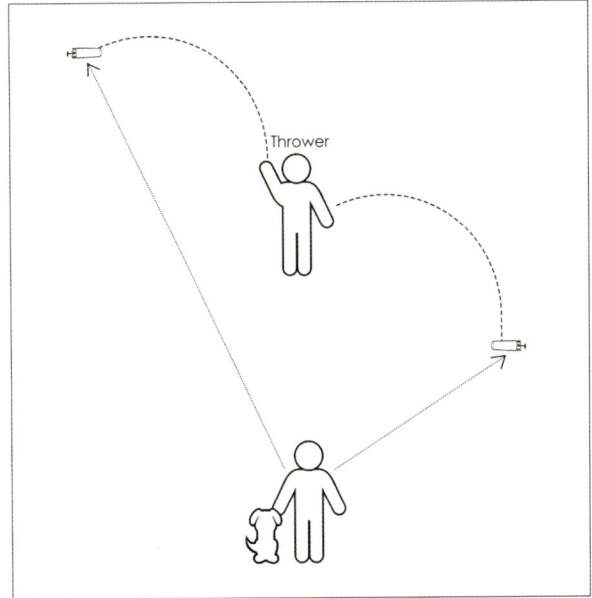

Angled marks are a better test of the dog's marking capability.

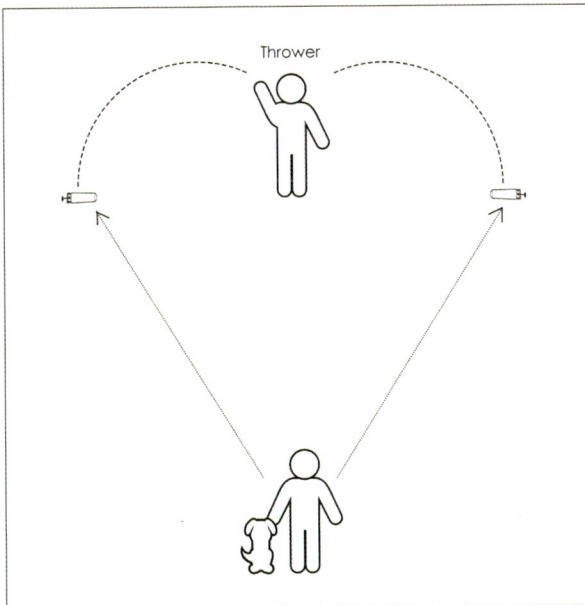

Typical 'flat' marks landing at the same depth as the thrower.

ficulty of retrieve. However, if they don't make it cleanly through those first round, short, markable retrieves, the rest is immaterial.

PICKING DOUBLE MARKS

Those training for working tests in particular will need to be able to pick double marks. In field trials, though, you don't usually get two retrieves in succession, unless you have just eye-wiped your running partner. As we discussed earlier, picking double marks will draw on the dog's ability to remember the second mark.

You can practise these doubles as a standard 'split' retrieve, where one dummy is thrown to the left and one to the right. Again, remember to vary the depth of the throw so that the dummies do not always land in line with the thrower. An important thing to remember when tackling these double marks is to treat each one as a single, and to face each squarely as it falls. This will give the dog that snapshot picture of each one individually, and will help with memory. A common mistake that people make with double 'split' marks is that they face themselves and their dog squarely looking at the thrower, and don't move as the marks go out. The dog then only has a 'half view' of the one on the right, from an angle, and the same for the left. This doesn't help the dog build an accurate picture of the fall of either. Turning the dog to face each mark, in turn, relies on good heelwork, as we discussed in Chapter 6. As soon as the handler moves to turn towards the mark, the dog should move with him to remain parallel at heel.

The other double marks are 'in-line' marks where the two dummies fall on the same line – one being short and the other long – and the short retrieve is picked first, regardless of the order in which they are thrown (so that the dog is not passing over game). It is worth practising this set-up periodically to teach the dog to gauge the differing distances accurately, and to practise retaining the mark of the long retrieve after the short one is picked, when he will be required to pass through the area of the first mark.

MARKING CHECKLIST

- **Turn towards the source of the mark (dummy thrower) not to the anticipated fall**

- **Track the dummy in the air, moving the dog at heel, to eventually face the fall squarely**

- **Mark the retrieve accurately yourself**

- **Monitor to ensure the dog has also marked the fall**

- **Ensure the dog meets all the criteria (steady, quiet, focused) for retrieving**

- **Vary the time before sending the dog to retrieve**

SCENT AND SCENTING CONDITIONS

It is widely understood that the dog's nose is far more sensitive than our own. Depending on which scientists you believe, dogs' olfactory receptors number into the hundreds of millions, whereas those of humans are in the single digit millions (Coren 2013). In addition, the area of the brain that is devoted to scent discrimination in dogs is also a lot larger than that of humans. To dogs, smell provides a network of information about their environment, including potential sources of food, danger and sex. Dogs make sense of their world through scent.

For a gundog in search of its quarry, it will be picking up on a cocktail of game scent, blood scent and shot scent. The way it does this will also vary from breed to breed. For example, Labradors are largely ground scenters, so will put their noses down to draw scent, whereas Golden Retrievers and Flatcoated Retrievers are air scenters, and will often be seen working the wind with a higher head carriage.

To be effective in taking in scent through the nasal passages, the dog needs to be travelling through an area at a deliberate and methodical pace, rather than racing around. Whilst speed is desirable to get the gundog quickly to the desired area to retrieve, it is the enemy when it comes to the dog being able to locate its quarry efficiently through scent. And we must remember that the dog is actually using its nose for two functions: breathing as well as detecting scent at the same time.

Ground type and weather can play a large part in affecting scenting conditions. Some types of crop have a distinctive smell, and others, such as heather, give off heavy blooms of pollen, which can make scenting difficult. Heavy clay soils that trap moisture at ground level are usually better for scenting than dry sandy soils. Bare ground, such as drill or grazed land, can also be notoriously difficult to hunt, not just because it doesn't trap scent, but more because a dog tends to switch to using its eyes in favour of its nose because it assumes it would see something in the open.

Hot, dry weather or extreme high winds can also make it very difficult for gundogs to catch scent. Ideal conditions seem to be moist air and some degree of wind, which helps to carry the scent molecules for the dog to pick them up via its nose. Awareness of the wind direction is important, not just from where the handler is

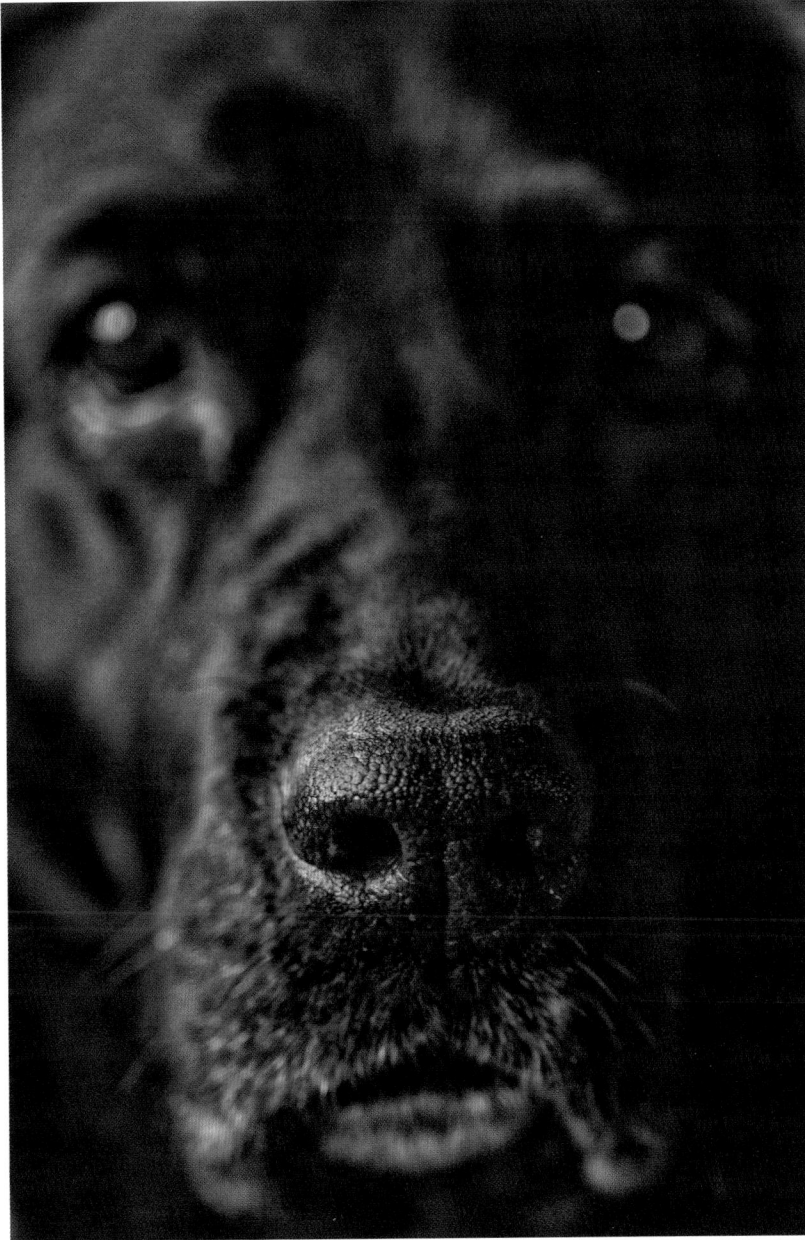

The dog's nose is hundreds of times more sensitive than our own, with the ability to detect tiny presences of scent.

bly woodcock and sometimes partridge, seem to have the ability to 'lock down' their scent when they have been wounded, so they are almost impossible to find. Likewise, there are times when a hare lying on the ground in roots, surrounded by shot scent, has proved challenging to pick, despite its size. Whether this is due to the soil type again (often sandy for beet crops) or the distraction of the shot scent, is uncertain.

Furthermore, when a retriever is sent for low shot game when walking up in root crops, it can get drawn away from the actual fall by the shotstring across the top of the beet. This can mean that as the dog reaches the fall to check down it suddenly darts away, which can lead the handler to thinking, mistakenly, that the dog is taking the line on a runner. Only when the dog is handled back to the fall area and picks there, is it apparent what has happened.

As handlers, we need to keep a watching brief when our dogs are working scent. There is an art in learning to read your own dog's body language as it touches scent, when it will demonstrate a distinct change in action. Try not to interfere – in particular there is no need to blow a hunt whistle or issue a hunt command if the dog is already hunting, because to do so will often distract the dog from its task.

standing, but where the dog is actually working. For example, the handler might be standing in an exposed field where there is a strong wind, but the dog may be working on the edge of a wood that is completely sheltered from any moving air.

In addition, a proliferation of game and wildlife scent on the ground can distract and confuse a dog in its scent work. And certain species, nota-

How are you feeling? Do you 'taste' upset or relaxed?

SCENT AS KEY IN GATHERING INFORMATION

Our dogs' noses and tongues are key tools in collecting information about us, too. It is often remarked that nerves seem to 'travel down the lead' at gundog competitions, and dogs sometimes end up behaving differently than they would at home or in training. It is likely that dogs pick up on our anxiety through body language (as discussed in Chapter 2), but this is also compounded by the scent of adrenalin, which we naturally secrete through our sweat. People have long talked of the 'smell of fear', which as humans we can no longer pick up on, with our own diminished sense of smell. But animals definitely do have a more acute sense of this. In this respect, to dogs, anxiety may have a smell.

A dog's sense of smell is also linked to that of taste, and we sometimes see dogs licking to 'test the waters'. An example of this is when a dog licks your hand after a communication with it. There is no common agreement as to why dogs lick us. The explanations range from trying to soothe us, and gathering information from our taste, through to the fact that we might just have scraps or the scent of food left on us. Some people feel that licking is an act of appeasement or subservience, while others believe that it is your dog's way of seeing exactly how you are feeling. Do you 'taste' cross, or do you 'taste' pleasant and relaxed? Is there a lot of adrenalin in the secretion from your hand, or is it neutral?

TAKING A RUNNER

The main *raison d'etre* of any retriever is the ability to retrieve the birds that cannot be picked by hand, primarily the 'runner' or injured game. This retrieving of wounded birds quickly and humanely is the most essential part of a gundog's work, but perhaps one of the hardest things to teach, as, unlike other aspects of training, it can only be done during the shooting season, on live game.

The only 'out of season' preparation you can give your dog to accustom it to the idea that sometimes retrieves will have moved is by letting it track a heavy ball that has been thrown and rolled down an incline. This will give the dog the basic mechanics of 'taking a line' on a runner. Set up this retrieve as a mark, where the dog is able to see the initial fall, but not able to see as the ball rolls further out of sight. Allow the dog to reach the fall and then leave him to it. Don't interfere with him, or attempt to blow a hunt whistle as this will only distract him. You want him to work things out using his own initiative and senses to locate the new position of the ball.

Tracking wounded game requires a degree of autonomy and self-reliance from the dog. He is working on his own natural instinct, using his nose to locate the quarry and follow its path. This is a skill that will be honed gradually over time when picking up on shoot days, when your dog will encounter all varieties of game.

Quickly locating and retrieving injured game is the primary role of the retriever. (Photo: Caroline Dell)

9 CONTROL

A good game-finding dog should not rely on the handler to find the game. It should, however, be obedient and respond to its handler's signals where necessary.

J(A)4g, KC Field Trial Regulations

In the previous chapter we looked at the importance of natural ability and how we can enhance this in our dogs, through teaching them to mark effectively. Now, we turn our attention to being able to handle our dogs efficiently to an area, directing them to retrieves that are unseen, or stepping in to handle them when they need support to find a retrieve.

Having a controlling nature seems to be a common theme amongst successful gundog trainers. Many of the personalities in the gundog world are quite strong-minded people. This is not always apparent on the surface, but if you get to know them, they are largely characterized as being fairly commanding or determined.

WHEN TO STEP IN

It is knowing when to use this control, and in turn, when to relinquish it, that forms the art of gundog training. With novice handlers, you often see people 'give up' when things get tough, or they will start to abdicate responsibility to their dogs. They become passengers, rather than drivers, when their dog goes out on a retrieve. Conversely, there are other handlers who step in and start controlling too soon, without giving the dog a chance to show any initiative or to recover the situation for itself, not allowing it to make decisions or learn as part of the training process.

Knowing exactly when to step in with handling, and how, comes with experience and is critical to success. Getting the balance right is part of the art of becoming an excellent handler.

It requires a strong partnership with the dog, as well as intelligence and biddability on the dog's part – to carry out commands but also to use its own natural ability when appropriate.

In handling work on blind retrieves, the dog shouldn't be making too many decisions on its own until it is engaged in hunting the correct area. It is your job as a handler to put the dog in a position to wind the bird or dummy, or to be able to work the area efficiently. However, it is not your job to 'put the dog on it', or to pick the bird for the dog. Let the dog do the work itself.

Equally, don't leave it to the dog to try and guess where the fall area might be if he hasn't seen it. So many handlers step in on a mark when the dog has mismarked, giving the dog some primary handling, but then tailing off and leaving the dog to guess what is required next. If you are handling, don't half-handle. Once you have stepped in to direct the dog, it is up to you to make the retrieve as efficient as possible from thereon, as you are now treating it as a blind. So, every cast and command should be aimed at getting your dog nearer to the area of the retrieve. Don't step in and then abandon the dog in the hope that he will then work it out on his own, even though he may be completely wrong for wind, or still a long way away from the area.

Although we will be dealing with aspects of control in this chapter, we will not be revisiting the rudimentary directional commands (left, right and back) that you have already gleaned from other books or trainers. The mechanics of these commands are fairly straightforward. Instead we will look at the different ways of sending for retrieves (lining), building drive and momentum, improving stops, and teaching methodical hunting.

Sending for a blind retrieve using a clear arm signal to line the dog.

DIFFERENTIATED SENDING

When sending your dog for a retrieve, consider how you send it, and what information you are giving the dog in your command. Are you using a vocal-only cue, or are you combining this with a hand signal or arm movement? Decide what you understand as the cue to retrieve, and then look at what your dog understands. For example, try using just your arm movement without your vocal command to send for a blind, and see if the dog goes. If the dog does move forwards, it may be that he understands the movement of your arm as his cue, rather than the vocal command. Neither is right or wrong, but you both need to be operating with the same understanding of the cues in a consistent manner.

Whereas you can send your dog for every retrieve with a single command, whether it is a blind or a marked retrieve, it is very useful to differentiate between these two types of retrieve by using separate commands. For example, many handlers send their dog for a mark on its name. This is particularly useful if you are working two dogs at a time, so each dog knows which is being sent for the retrieve that it has just seen. Using the name 'releases' the correct dog for the mark that it has seen. Then for a blind you can use a different command, such as 'go back', combined with an arm signal to indicate direction.

Using separate commands for the two types of retrieve gives the dog additional information, and provides clarity in a situation of multiple retrieves. For example, the dog has marked a retrieve directly ahead of it (using a clock face, at twelve o'clock), but you are asked to pick a blind retrieve on a tight angle (say, at two o'clock). By turning the dog at heel to face the blind, and by then using your blind command, you are effectively saying to the dog: 'It's a blind in that direction', so the dog knows not to go for the mark it has just seen. This removes the need to point at the mark and say 'leave that', before then re-lining the dog for the blind that you do want. If you use the same command for both a mark and a blind, then the difference would be less clear, as you would just be saying 'go and get it', and the dog might think that the slight difference in angle is just you pointing a bit off course – in this instance the dog will be more likely to use its initiative to pull for the mark that it has seen.

Consider the two different sendaways as follows:

- **Releasing** the dog for a mark: it has seen it and knows where it is going
- **Sending** the dog for a blind: it is being told to run in a particular direction until the next instruction

For a delayed mark (where the dog and handler have remained in the same position, but some time has elapsed before sending), use your mark command, but indicate the direction of the mark with your hand. This command is saying to the dog 'go and get *that* mark that you saw earlier'.

At this point it is useful to clear up any confusion over what constitutes a mark and memory mark versus a blind, for the purposes of training. If we think of a dummy being thrown in the air and we take a photographic snapshot of it from the point where we are standing, we have a perfect picture of it, which shows us the line as well as the depth in relation to other landscape features. This is a mark. Now imagine that some time has elapsed, perhaps with another dog being sent for a different retrieve, and then we are asked to take this retrieve. We can refer back to our snapshot, because nothing has changed. The line is the same, and the depth, and all the points of reference – so we can treat this retrieve as a mark as well (a memory mark).

Next, we are told to move fifty yards back to make the retrieve longer, or we are taken to the other end of the line, so we are shifted to the right by forty yards. If we pick up our photographic image now, it doesn't relate to how we now see the area of the retrieve from our new location. In the first instance the depth has altered, and in the second the angle has altered. In both of these situations, the retrieve should now be treated as a blind. Some people might still (wrongly) call them 'memory marks', but they are perhaps better termed as 'memory blinds', in that the dog has a memory of a retrieve having gone out to a rough area, but it has no longer got that locked-on focused picture to work with. It has confidence that there is something out there (which can be used to support its work on blinds), but it no longer has an accurate reference of the location.

RETRIEVE SCENARIOS

Think about the individual commands you use to cue the dog to retrieve, and how you treat multiple retrieves using these commands. When competing in working tests, or working in the field, the following are the likely combinations of retrieves that you might get, and the send commands.

MARKS

Single mark: When the dog is definitely 'locked on' to the mark, you can release it with a voice-only mark command.

'Unmarkable' single mark: The mark may be thrown at long distance or obscured by terrain or trees; the dog may only have 'marked' the shot, rather than seen the fall. Use the vocal mark command, but combine it with an arm signal to indicate direction. This way you are reinforcing that it was a mark, in case he did see it, and confirming the direction of travel. In these cases it is difficult for the dog to have an accurate concept of the precise area of the fall.

Split double mark: (Where the last thrown dummy is picked first.) As the dummies are thrown out, turn to face each one so that the dog locks on and retains a strong visual picture of each mark. Release the dog on the vocal mark command for the last dummy down, as it will be focused on this. Once that is picked, turn to the first dummy, and send using the mark command with voice and arm indicating direction. This is a straight mark followed by a memory mark.

Split double mark: (Where the first thrown dummy is picked first.) As above, turn the dog to face each mark as it is thrown. Turn back towards the first thrown dummy and release the dog using the mark command, with voice and arm indicating direction. Then do the same for the second dummy. These are two memory marks.

In-line double mark: In this scenario, with the two dummies being on the same line, you can release with just the voice for the mark, if the dog has locked on. You may have to step in to hold the dog on to the short dummy, to stop it powering over it to the second dummy, depending on the order in which they were thrown, and how well the dog has marked the depth of each. For the second retrieve, you will release the dog with a vocal mark command and arm signal, as this will be a memory mark.

BLINDS

Blind (single or double): Use the blind vocal command and arm signal to send the dog.

COMBINATIONS

In-line mark, then blind: Release the dog for the mark using the vocal mark command only (if it is locked on), and then send it for the blind with the blind command and arm signal. Because the dog understands the blind command, it should power through the area of the former mark without hesitating as it knows it is just running in a line for a blind. There is no confusion about it going back to the area of the mark.

In-line blind, then mark: How you tackle this scenario may depend on the type of dog that you have. Where you are asked to pick a blind that is on the way to a mark at a further distance, you can release the dog on the marked command to use the attraction of the mark to pull out a less confident dog or less driven dog. Then use a stop whistle to stop the dog in the correct area to hunt for the blind. This is better than lining for a blind using your blind command towards the mark, which can cause confusion and lack of drive in this type of dog, as it deals with the conflicting information of being told it is a blind, but being pointed directly at the mark.

Conversely, with a more headstrong dog, you may decide to line for the blind using the blind sendaway to indicate to him that you

A white dummy placed out as a 'trailing memory blind' down a track provides a strong target for the dog to run to, in its build-up work to true blinds.

will be controlling him to pick something that is unseen. Then for both types of dog, the mark would be a memory mark, meaning that you would indicate direction with your arm signal and release the dog on the mark command.

Blind with mark diversion at an angle: Turn to mark the seen retrieve, and take your time to let the dog lock on and retain the picture of the mark. Then deliberately turn towards the blind and cue the dog for the blind retrieve, with the blind vocal command and arm signal. Once that is picked, turn back to take the marked retrieve, using the vocal mark command with the arm signal to confirm the direction of travel.

BUILDING BLINDS

Unlike the marked retrieve, there is no natural draw for a dog to run out with pace towards a blind. There is no visual stimulus of seeing a bird or dummy in the air to promote the desire to chase. Blind work is not an innate skill in the dog, but requires methodical training. It is necessary to build confidence in the dog, as you are sending him out for something that he hasn't seen, and therefore he needs to have complete trust in you that there is a retrieve in the direction that you are sending him. This trust is gradually instilled over time as the dog learns the cues and patterns that eventually inform his work on true blinds.

In the early stages of building towards blinds you will use remembered placed or thrown dummies to maintain the dog's confidence, as he knows that there is something in the area you are sending him towards. With a young dog, do 'trailing memory blinds': throw or drop a dummy behind you, on a track or along a fence line, then walk away to a point from where the dog will be able to remember where the dummy is, or can see it (it is useful to use white or contrast dummies that are highly visual on short grass, so that the dog can lock on to his target when he is sent back). Then turn round and send the dog back using your blind command. It is really important to go through the exact cues that you eventually want to use for your blind sendaway, as you are using this exercise to build confidence in true blinds when the time eventually comes. Don't be

too rushed in your sendaway, but take your time instead to get the dog focused on the line he will run.

Once the dog is powering out with confidence on these single memory blinds, you can start to build in differentiation by sending him to two different locations. Until this point your sendaway command has just meant 'run' to the dog, as he has a clear idea that the dummy is in the area you have just walked directly away from. Now you must teach him that the hand signal means run in a particular direction, as opposed to any direction. You can lay out dummies in a triangle at 90 degrees, or directly opposing each other at 180 degrees, and practise turning the dog to them and sending him to each in turn.

Eventually you will build to more acute angles on the clockface, and will require a more precise line. Good heelwork will make your turning straightforward at this point, and with the dog's body parallel to your own, all you will need to do is put your arm down in the direction of the dummy so that the dog can lock on to its target (again a visual dummy), and send him with your blind command.

PROMOTING DRIVE

All your early work on teaching blinds should be about building confidence and drive. The training is focused on the dog taking the command and driving hard towards the target area. Once he reaches the area, he should pick quickly and easily. Either use highly visual dummies on bare ground, or 'seed' the area with several dummies, if your grass is longer, so that he will reach the area and wind or fall over a retrieve when he gets there. Later on you can address accuracy of line, but it is a big mistake to focus on this too early. A useful adage to remember at this stage is: *focus on momentum and accuracy will arrive, focus on accuracy and momentum will depart.* It is very easy to squash confidence and repress drive by being too specific on the accuracy of line. In the early stages, be prepared to accept just running and making a distance. Later on, you can address the need for greater accuracy of line.

Memory blinds form a large part of building confidence in the set-up for true blinds. They

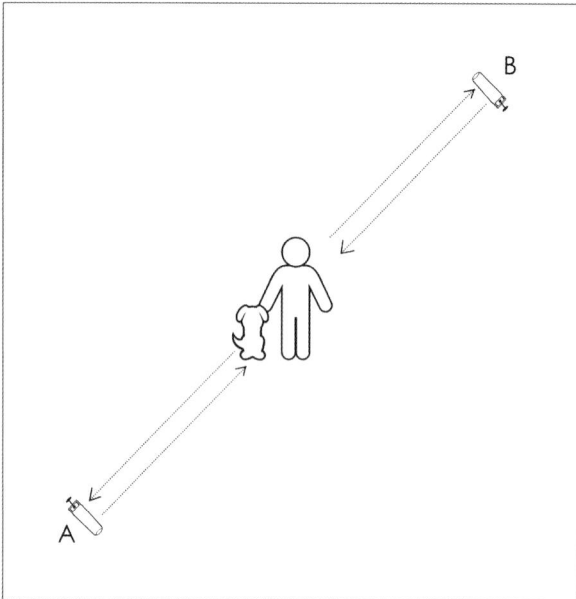

A 180-degree trailing memory blind. Walk out to A with the dog and place the dummy, then walk out to B with the dog and place the second dummy. Send the dog to A, and then send it to B.

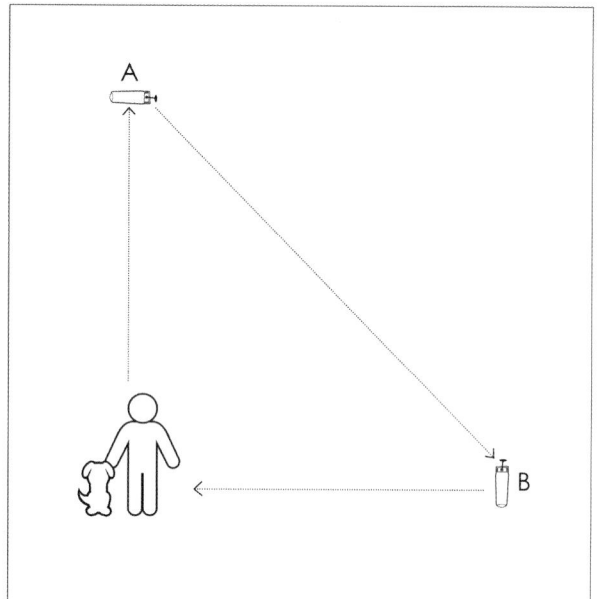

Triangle walk memory blind. Walk with the dog to A and place the dummy, then from there to B and place the second dummy, and from there back to the start position. Send the dog to A, and then send it to B.

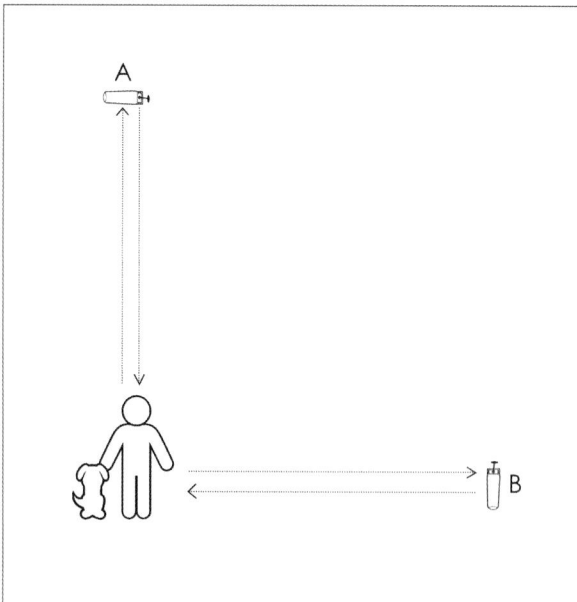

A 90-degree trailing memory blind. The set-up is the same as the 180-degree version, but now the arm signal is more significant in indicating the direction of travel.

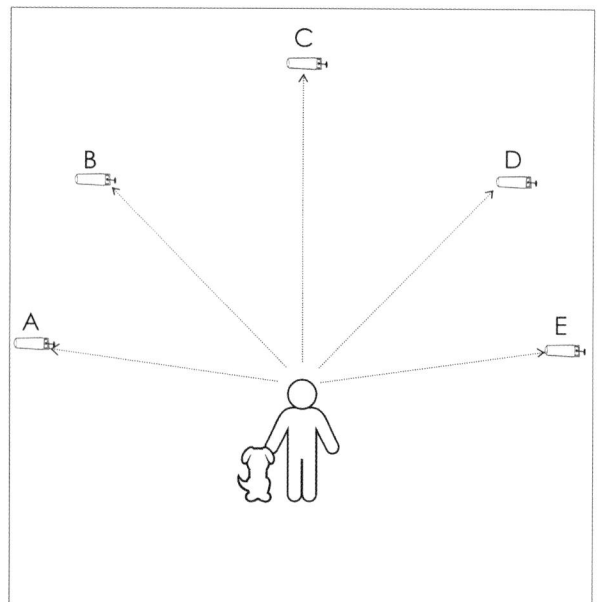

Clock-face drill. Place the dummies at positions A to E, and then send the dog in turn for each, starting from A initially. Once the dog has achieved this accurately, then you can send it in reverse order, or randomly.

CASE STUDY: RESOLVING 'POPPING' AND SPINNING ON THE OUTRUN

Background: Evie, a two-year-old Labrador, was extremely biddable and wanted to work with her handler, but lacked confidence on blinds.

Issue: As her training had progressed, Evie would run out on a blind retrieve but would check back with her handler at a distance of about forty to fifty metres. At first, because of previous experience with a 'hard-headed' dog, her handler was delighted that Evie wanted to engage and was asking for help, rather than just continuing on her own. She didn't realize that this would become a problem as the dog reached Open level competition and was required to work at greater distances, and to a higher standard. So she had let it continue for a while to the point that her 'popping' (stopping and looking at the handler without being asked) became a habit; moreover sometimes Evie would also spin on the line out to the retrieve.

Action: We used a multi-pronged approach to resolve the issue:

- I suggested a separate command for the blind sendaway, as the handler was previously using one command for both marks and blinds. This was causing anxiety with the dog as it hadn't seen a mark, so was unsure that it should go. Using a new command for a blind, and building it from scratch, put a firm framework in place for the dog to be confident in its cue and what it meant
- We did plenty of 'easy' memory blinds to visible dummies or to 'comfort areas' to increase Evie's confidence, and stretched the distance beyond her usual stopping distance. Sometimes we worked over the brow of the hill so that the dummy was out of sight on the first twenty to thirty metres, but then came into sight just before Evie dried up or lost momentum
- We were strict about keeping things simple, and therefore gaining multiple 'wins'. We kept a tick chart of every time the dog did an outrun without popping, and aimed for ten out of ten on each training outing. This removed the temptation to test the dog or push it a little too far, as the handler couldn't put a tick on the chart if there was a single failure
- We introduced praise to endorse only the strong outruns so the dog was rewarded for the exact behaviour we wanted
- We remembered to have fun and still include marks in the training. When you have an issue like this, it is very hard not to fixate on it; by doing so, you often forget to do the 'easy' exercises that the dog enjoys and can do. Training can become dull for the dog if you keep repeating the same set-ups. Also, by giving the dog plenty of marks, where the dog runs out confidently, in between the memory blind work, you are practising success and building muscle memory for not stopping, sticking or spinning. The more times the dog does the outrun strongly and correctly, the more it will become a new habit

Result: After continued and consolidated effort, keeping to a routine of ensuring that the work was simple and achievable, and only moving on in very small increments, the handler was able to break the habit and the dog was eventually completing long outruns without stopping.

will help you maintain drive and the dog's belief. If you need to build added excitement into this work, try the following: throw out your memory blind with the dog at your side, then run back together to the area you will send from, spin round, hold the dog a little in the sendaway position (to build tension/anticipation), then send him straight back. This should have the dog driving back hard to the area.

As the dog matures, memory blinds should still form an important aspect of your training, as they will help you to reinforce line work across difficult terrain as well as maintaining confidence. It is a mistake to move on too quickly to work on 'true' blinds – pushing the dog or testing it – before it has strong momentum. This can damage the dog's trust and will affect its attitude to blind work. A dog that is not confident in its line work will either suffer lack of momentum from the onset of sendaway – in some cases not going at all – or it will go out to a short distance and falter or stop and ask for help. These habits, once they are ingrained, are tricky to resolve and it will take a lot of remedial work to rebuild drive in the outrun.

COMBINING LINE WORK WITH HANDLING

Once your line work has been built strongly, you can begin to combine it with the static direction work that you have been working on separately. Starting this 'joined up' handling work is a big step, and is the beginning of everything coming together so you can successfully handle your dog on to any blind retrieve.

Up until this point, when you are working on running a line, don't attempt to step in and handle in order for the dog to reach the dummy. If it has not made the distance from the initial sendaway, call the dog back and reset the exercise, either trying again, or, if necessary, simplifying the exercise so the dog can achieve the retrieve in one single cast. If you step in with handling at this stage, it is likely to become a pattern, and the dog will begin to rely on you to handle it out towards a retrieve, rather than taking the initial command and continuing to run.

When you begin adding directional commands to handle the dog to the dummy, it is likely that the dog will not take each command perfectly in this new regime. This can be due to a number of factors, but commonly it is one of the following: lack of familiarity with new ground; lack of belief/confidence that there is a retrieve in that direction; not wanting to face the wind or difficult cover; the draw of another retrieve elsewhere; not understanding or being unfamiliar

with the command.

Depending on the type of dog you are working with, and how you have set up the retrieve, you can use one of the approaches discussed in Chapter 4, when the dog does not take the cast. These are attrition, feedback leading to correction, and letting the dog take the 'wrong' cast (choice leading to 'extinction').

Attrition

Stop the dog (using the whistle command) and move it to regain the ground it has taken in, by recalling it and handling it back to where the initial cast was given; then repeat the command until the dog takes it. This may take several attempts, but eventually the dog will try the cast and be rewarded. The learning taken from this by the dog is that it has tried other options and not gained success, but when it listened to the handler, and followed his instruction, it found the retrieve.

Feedback/Correction

Vocally mark the dog's failed cast with a correction 'no', and go out and put the dog back in position, resetting it to try the cast again. The learning from this approach is negative, in that the dog has tried something and has received negative feedback for it (correction for going 'wrong'). This can have a flattening effect on the dog and it may be reluctant to try again. This method should only be used with caution, and not with dogs that lack initiative or self-confidence.

Choice/Extinction

Let the dog take the 'wrong' cast and watch what happens next. This method can only be used if there are no other retrieves out in other directions, so the dog cannot 'self-reward' by finding something else using its own initiative. After the dog has tried under its own initiative, you will see it starting to run out of ideas and slow down its efforts. Wait for the dog to look as if it wants to re-engage with you. At this point you have two options. You can either walk out and collect the dog and put it back at the initial point you gave it the refused cast. Or you can stop the dog with the whistle and handle it back to the original cast

Once lining is established, you can begin to combine this with directional commands.

and learning through patterns. Over time, the dog will learn to put his trust in you, particularly if he can't find the retrieves without your input.

To use this method of training you will need to be thoughtful in your placement and picking of retrieves so that when the dog does go wrong, it cannot self-reward. This is absolutely critical, and if you get it wrong, it will undermine your training.

START WITH STOP TRAINING

Unlike some trainers, I prefer to have the stop in place before I start the 'go' work. Because of the early conditioning work that I have done around the house with the young puppy (*see* Chapter 5), it understands the stop whistle from an early age, and that it means something really positive and rewarding. I continue this work on stops in the field, by prefacing all of my static cast work (left, right and back) with a stop whistle. So the sequence is as follows:

1. Leave the dog remotely in the field in the position from which you want to cast.
2. Return to your position, facing it at an appropriate distance.
3. Blow the stop whistle – at which point the dog should look at you.

area to repeat the command. In either case, the dog has now satisfied its curiosity, checking that the dummy wasn't where it thought it was, and is now ready to work with the handler. It will be more receptive to your input.

The latter option – choice/extinction – may seem somewhat counter-intuitive in allowing the dog to continue to work on its own, 'disobeying' a given command, but it is worth persevering, and thinking about the learning to be taken by the dog. Focus on the training process. In this instance, the dog doesn't take the command, and it doesn't get a reward (the retrieve). It wasn't the outcome that you wanted from issuing the command, but it also wasn't a positive outcome for the dog. You directed the dog to go one way, but it trusted its own ideas over your own, and went with that – and it didn't work. However, there was no harm in letting the dog find out for himself that he wouldn't get very far without listening to you. Dogs are good at recognizing

119

4. Praise it for that eye contact, and then cast it towards the dummy that you have placed or thrown out.

In this way, the cast to the retrieve rewards the 'stop' and eye contact. Quickly the stop whistle is reinforced as meaning 'stop, and look at me because something great is about to happen'. It is the key to gaining a reward, rather than something that is punitive or prevents a dog from achieving a retrieve.

Several years ago I had a group of trainers here from Sweden. They had young dogs that were all about two years old. And they told me that they hadn't yet started using the stop whistle, although they had been using a hunt whistle. So their dogs could do marked retrieves on their own, and they had 'run' and 'hunt', but no brakes and steering. They had power and style, but were relying almost solely on their own natural ability. But it was now time, the handlers felt, that they should be introducing the stop whistle. But when they tried, it was met with a lot of resistance from the dogs, and problems ensued. The dogs had always been able to do as they pleased, so when the handler now tried to step in, his 'help' was seen as an intrusion and an unwelcome interrupter to what the dog was already doing for itself. The dog was not accustomed to intervention or help, and it didn't have a concept of what a positive benefit stopping and handling could be. The dog resented the stop whistle.

It is much easier to introduce the stop whistle in a positive way into early training, than leaving it until later, when the dog has matured and gained more opinions about how to behave. Of course, the initial puppy 'stops', done at feed times and at short range in the garden, will have to be generalized to new locations and distances. But the concept will already be imbedded into the dog's behaviour, so this transition should be relatively smooth.

IMPROVING THE STOP WHISTLE

When you want to work on improving the stop whistle, perhaps because it has become sloppy (with the dog 'running on' or taking in a few steps before stopping) or the dog's natural instincts are taking over and it fails to stop, look for 'safe' areas to stop the dog. This means, when you set up a retrieve, work out where you can stop the dog where there will be no opportunity for it to find the dummy if it doesn't stop. You will need to consider the wind direction, so that the dog doesn't wind the retrieve, and also the proximity to the retrieve, if it is liable to start hunting frantically rather than stopping directly. You need to be sure that there will not be the opportunity for the dog to reward itself if it fails to stop, but that you will be able to reward it if it does.

If you know that your stop whistle requires work, look for the chance to handle in this way, don't avoid it. It may look impressive and be satisfying to pick a memory retrieve in a single cast, but save that for the trial, test or shoot day. In training, be proactive about using opportunities to ensure a reliable stop whistle. I am always on the lookout for these 'stopportunities' in training to make sure that I remain in contact with my dog. You can still work on lining and reaching a distance in a single sendaway. So instead of lining directly from A to B, consider lining from A to C, stopping the dog there, and casting to B. This means you are still working on your straight line to an area, but you now have the added elements of stop and cast, too.

THE LESS-THAN-PERFECT STOP WHISTLE

As you tighten up your stop-whistle work, consider using a sliding scale, to deal with less-than-perfect stop whistles. For example, if you are starting with a dog that takes several steps before stopping, then that is your baseline. If this dog takes fewer steps after hearing the whistle, and then stops, you can accept this as an improvement, but don't reward it. If it stops tightly another time, then you can reward it (vocally and by using a retrieve, or by going out and delivering praise or a food reward). If the dog fails to stop, or still offers the same extremely poor version of stop, then you can go out and collect the dog, repositioning it where you issued the stop command, reinforcing the command, and then carrying on. Gradually the dog will start to see the pattern, and will learn what gains it a reward.

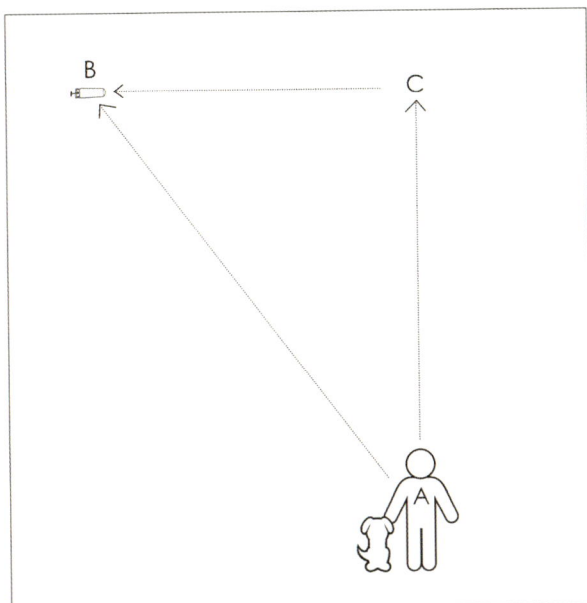

Send the dog from A to C and stop it. If it stops promptly, you can then cast it to B to retrieve the dummy as a reward. If it does not stop, then it is unable to self-reward as there is no dummy placed at C. (Note: the wind direction should be from right to left, so that the dog does not wind the dummy at B when it gets to C.)

Stopping the dog before it enters a wood is sometimes useful so that the initial outrun speed has been slowed, and you can push the dog back to precisely where you want it (left- or right-handed).

KEEP THE STOP WHISTLE SEPARATE

Remember to ensure that you keep the stop whistle separate from your next command, and that it doesn't become confused with it. This is particularly important when you stop the dog and then go on to hunt it on a whistle command. Make a pause between the stop whistle and the hunt command, otherwise the dog will start to see a pattern whereby the stop whistle comes to mean that he must be in the right area to find a retrieve, and that he should start hunting there anyway because he will find something. Putting a pause in, in training, between the stop whistle and the next command, also gives the dog time to 'cool its head' and collect itself, before taking on board the information given in the next command. You don't want it rushing off again without thinking and fully assimilating what it is being told.

STOPPING THE FAST DOG

If you have a very fast dog, consider using a stop whistle before he actually reaches the area of the retrieve – that is, stop him short of the retrieve and then 'bounce' him back the last few yards. This is useful to kill some of the speed of the initial outrun, and means that when you push the dog back the remaining distance he is travelling more slowly and is under better control. There is, therefore, more likelihood of him winding the retrieve as he passes into the area, than if he were travelling at full speed. Also, stopping the dog short means you avoid the scenario above whereby the dog believes he is now in the area and starts to hunt on his own initiative. Or, in the event of him not stopping, he will be less likely to pick the retrieve as he has not yet reached the correct area.

THE INFLUENCE OF TERRAIN

Also, think about the terrain in the retrieve, and where it might be useful to stop the dog. For example, if the retrieve is a blind out of sight ten metres over the brow of a hill, it would be best to stop the dog at the last point that he will be in sight, before he goes over the brow of the hill. In this way, you will be able to see his position in relation to where the retrieve is, and adjust

In response to the stop whistle, it doesn't matter if the dog stands or sits, as long as its attention is focused on the handler.

his line if necessary before you push him back so that he will be right to wind the retrieve. If you send him from your side and don't stop him until he is out of sight, you won't know where he is in relation to the retrieve when he stops (if he stops!), and his speed may take him too far out of the area once he is out of sight.

STOP, NOT SIT

Finally, the stop whistle is just that – 'stop'. It doesn't need to mean that the dog should sit. Some dogs naturally spin up into a sit (I've seen this trait more in Golden Retrievers than Labradors, but wouldn't like to say that it is a breed trait, or whether it is produced by a difference in training methods). Other dogs prefer to stand. As long as they look at you, and are ready for their next instruction, it doesn't matter. Too many times I've seen nice stops negated by handlers shouting at their poor dogs to 'sit, sit' and getting cross, when the dog has actually produced a nice positive stop/stand and turn to face the handler. It has done the right thing, but the handler is insistent on a sit as well, and so it becomes quite negative or punitive for the dog.

HUNTING

The main purpose of any gundog is game finding. While spaniels are used primarily for hunt-

ing and flushing game for the gun, retrievers are mainly used to find injured or dead quarry, and bring it back to hand. This should be done quickly and efficiently. Hunting is an innate and instinctive trait in a gundog, and natural ability is of primary importance, but you also need to be able to control your dog in its quest, so that it doesn't unduly disturb too much ground in the process. Ideally you want to send your dog quickly to an area and ask it to hunt there to find game.

There are three key stimuli that give the retriever a reason to hunt: sight, scent and command. Firstly, seeing is believing. A visual stimulus, such as watching a bird fall into an area of cover, will give a retriever a very strong incentive to hunt that area. Secondly, when the dog catches scent, it will want to check that out. The dog's world is largely scent driven and we know that their noses are thousands of times more developed than our own in detecting and identifying scent. Finally, once a signal is taught and understood, the dog will hunt an area on command. Eventually this will be the only cue that the dog needs to make it hunt in a given area.

TEACHING TO HUNT ON COMMAND

The process of teaching a retriever to hunt as directed can be achieved in several ways. Some trainers like to link the chosen hunt command – be it a whistle or word – to the activity of hunting when the dog is out already hunting on a marked retrieve. This is learning by association of doing, whereby the dog is engaged in the process of hunting, and is fully committed to it, and the handler adds in (or back-chains) the hunt command, so that eventually the dog makes the association between what it was doing and the command. It is practising success in that the dog has already got the activity right – hunting in the area of a retrieve.

The possible down side of this method is that it can lead to some dogs becoming over whistle reliant on a mark, whereby they expect to hear the command in the area before they pick. This may mean that they wait for the command to hunt, relying on the handler, when they should just be getting on with the job on their own. Also, I have seen this over-use of the hunt com-

mand lead to dogs standing over game before picking – a major fault. Because they haven't heard the command, they are not sure whether they are allowed to go ahead and pick the game on their own without the hunt command.

I prefer to teach the hunt command as a standalone exercise, not off the back of a marked retrieve. I teach it from a static position, as this would be the starting point for hunting once the dog had reached the area. Working from close quarters in a stationary position also means that you have killed any speed from the outrun, and puts the dog in a calm and level-headed position to begin an efficient hunt.

Tennis balls are ideal to use for hunting practice. They are cheap, readily available and just small enough to sit in longer grass and be obscured. You can also buy smaller, heavy dummies, discs or rubber balls, which drop right down into cover and are harder to find than a standard dummy.

Firstly, sit or stand the dog in your chosen area, usually a patch of longer grass. Allow the dog to watch you throw a tennis ball into the area immediately around him, and make sure it is just obscured. Repeat this process, so that there are a couple of balls in the area within a metre or two of the dog. Take into consideration the wind direction in the placement of the balls in relation to the dog. In this instance you want him to be downwind of the retrieve so that he is getting scent up his nose already, from where he is sitting. The sight and scent of the retrieve items will be a powerful support to the dog when it is asked to hunt. Stay close to the dog. Then use your chosen hunt command, which the dog won't understand at this point, as well as some body language in the form of arm movement to indicate where the balls are. So in my case it would be 'pip, pip' on the whistle, and when the dog doesn't move, just encouraging him to find the retrieve, helping him with a low arm movement towards the ground.

Repeat this a number of times, re-setting the tennis balls periodically so that the visual stimulus remains high to support the dog's understanding of what is required. In the early stages of this exercise the dog will need quite a bit of body movement and visual support, but gradually he

When you first start teaching the hunt command, the dog will require body language, such as an arm movement to indicate the area, to support his hunting.

will come to realize that the sound of the whistle is his cue to start hunting. Stay with the dog all the time, helping him to succeed and making this an enjoyable game.

Progressing the Exercise
The progression of this exercise is to drop out one or other of the support stimuli. So next you might let the dog see you place a ball in the area, but he will be wrong for wind (the dog will be upwind of the ball). Now the dog will be operating on the visual stimulus plus the command cue. You can also move further away from the dog, so he is facing you now at a short distance.

When the dog is more confident, remove the visual stimulus but put the dog in a downwind situation, so that he is touching a bit of scent but hasn't seen you place the ball. Some trainers use shot scent from a starting pistol fired into the ground to hold the dog in the area. I don't like to do this, as I don't want my dog fixing on ground shot scent over and above the scent of the retrieve item. This time the dog is working on scent stimulus and again the command cue. Eventually you will be working towards the dog being able to hunt solely on command, without the other cues. This means that you can put the dog in any area and give it the hunt command, and it will immediately put its nose down and begin hunting.

The Last Stage
Pay attention, at this last stage, to what exactly is cueing the dog to hunt. You want him to be operating on the aural signal of either the whistle or voice, and not looking for supporting body language in the form of an arm drawing him down. This is useful if your dog is unsighted in a wood or high crop, and will hunt purely on the heard command.

Once your dog is confident in its understanding of the hunt command, try prefacing these exercises with the stop whistle. This reinforces the stop whistle in a positive way, in that the dog knows that the stop whistle means that something exciting is about to happen in the form of its next command. So it will be riveted to you with its eyes and ears, waiting for the go-ahead to launch into the hunt.

The Hunt Area
When you work on this static hunting exercise, have an idea of what you think is a reasonable hunt area. For me, this is roughly a circle of about six metres diameter maximum. But, everyone's views on this will differ. However, bear in mind that dogs will naturally open up their area on a hunt rather than close it down, especially on game. So, it is better to teach them to hold as tight an area as possible initially, so that they treat the ground thoroughly around them.

Look for a Low Pace
Also, look for a low pace. You don't want the dog roaring over the ground using loads of brawn but not actually applying itself diligently. Speed is not your friend with hunting, as the faster dogs are often travelling too quickly over the ground for them to take in scent efficiently. They look stylish and flashy, but quite often don't find, whereas the slower paced dog will, with its more methodical treatment of the ground.

The Directional Hunt Command
Later on, the hunt cue can be combined with a directional cue when you know where your dog is in relation to a specific retrieve. For example, if the area you want to hunt is just to the right of your dog it will be more efficient to ask him to hunt right, rather than to just let him hunt the area where he has stopped with no directional input from you.

My directional hunt command is the same whistle signal, but with the arm half-extended held in the direction I want, with no body or arm movement. Depending on wind direction, if the dog is within five metres of the retrieve I will hunt him directionally to it, rather than casting him to it. This is an important point. Using directional hunting for short movements left or right means that you can reserve your casting for large direction changes. In this way, you are not weakening your casting by using it for short distance manoeuvres. Try to reserve pure casts for distances greater than ten metres (depending on wind conditions).

Hunt left: the ball is placed in cover to the side of the dog, and the handler has a low left arm signal to show the desired direction of hunt, without it being a full cast left.

more practice is needed.

Also, don't keep repeating the hunt command to the dog while he is working. Remember, as we said before, aim for a 'one command response'. Instead, support the dog in the early stages of his learning with feedback for his efforts. Let me use an analogy to explain why here.

You have been employed as a filing clerk, and in the morning, you start your task of sorting and filing a huge tray of paperwork for your manager. Periodically, your boss comes over to check on how you are doing. Boss A comes over and just says 'Do the filing, do the filing'. And you think to yourself, but I *am* doing the filing! I'm doing it as well as I can. I can't do any more than I am already doing! That boss keeps reiterating these instructions on each visit and you start to feel disheartened and rather pressurized. Conversely, in the same scenario, Boss B comes over to you and says, 'Well done, Bob. You're doing a great job. I can see that you are really putting in a lot of effort and thought to that job. That's brilliant.' Your efforts are recognized and rewarded, and you feel a bit of a glow about the work that you are carrying out, knowing you are doing well, and that your effort is appreciated. Who would you rather carry on working for?

As we discussed in Chapter 4, behaviours that are rewarded are more likely to be repeated. So it is up to us to notice when our dogs are doing the things we like, and feed back to them that what they are doing is great. When I am teaching my dog to hunt, and he shows me a really stylish and methodical hunt, holding the area, I will quietly

AIM FOR A 'ONE COMMAND RESPONSE'

Once a dog has started on the hunt exercise, don't complicate the issue by adding in extra commands. Stick to what you are trying to teach it. For example, if the dog moves too far out of the area, don't stop it and re-direct it back to the area again, because that would turn the hunting exercise into a handling exercise as well. This would leave you with another problem, if the dog then doesn't also handle correctly. Try to work on just the one training element at a time – in this case hunting. Keep to the task in hand. With this in mind, if the dog moves away, just go and collect him, take him back to the area – re-setting the exercise – and start again with your hunt command. This is effectively saying to the dog 'I've asked you to hunt there. Trust me. I know it is in this area.' If the dog is moving out of the area it is just a sign that it doesn't yet fully understand what the command means, and support him with a little vocal praise, to let him know that I like his behaviour. Over time, and as his behaviour becomes confident and fully conditioned in all aspects, this can also be phased out, so that the dog is not relying on it to keep hunting. Thus I move gradually from commentary to quiet, as the dog needs to learn to do it without vocal support. This is all part of the process from teaching to taught.

As the hunt command becomes more ingrained, and the hunting pattern is consistent, you can add more distance between yourself and the dog in the hunt area. Next, you can link it to other commands, such as recall to hunt area, stop and hunt, and outrun to hunt area, stop and hunt.

Preface the Hunt Command with a Stop Whistle
When I am eventually working the dog in the field, I always preface the hunt command with a stop whistle. This is to anchor the dog in the right area, to kill the speed of the outrun, and to ensure that he is focused on me ready for my next instruction. When a dog is running out from the initial sendaway, he is likely to be travelling at some speed. I liken this to being in sixth gear in a car. Speed to get him quickly to the fall is essential for an efficient retrieve. But speed is the enemy when I then ask the dog to hunt, as he will pass over game if he is travelling around the area too fast. So I want him to start in low gear again for this task.

However, with a slower paced dog, there are times when you may want to hunt him 'on the run' to avoid making him look too pedestrian and sticky. In this case, with this type of dog, you try and maintain the flow – but in general, stopping a dog in the area first will give him the best chance of finding the retrieve.

10 BARRIERS AND BUNKERS

By prevailing over all obstacles and distractions, one may unfailingly arrive at his chosen goal or destination.

Christopher Columbus, explorer

As retriever training reaches the more advanced stages, particularly for those who are competing in working tests or field trials, dogs will be required to negotiate challenges in order to achieve their retrieves. In addition to increased distances, the dogs will have to traverse a variety of terrain and cover, and natural or man-made barriers such as fences, dry-stone walls, dykes, ditches, streams, lakes and gullies. Throughout these varied scenarios, handlers should be looking for the most efficient retrieve, whereby the dog goes quickly and directly from A to B without making unnecessary diversions from its route.

NEGOTIATING AN OBSTACLE

The most commonly used command given to a retriever to negotiate an obstacle in its path is 'get over'. Handlers will often use this command when a dog reaches a fence or ditch, or a stretch of water. But what does the dog understand from this command? It is worth giving this some thought.

When a handler says 'get over' as the dog approaches a fence or wall, if the command is taught and understood successfully, then the dog should associate the vocal command with jumping over that obstacle in its path. As the dog approaches the obstacle, the handler commands 'get over' and the dog jumps. However, handlers also use 'get over' for crossing water, and in this instance they are not expecting the dog to jump on this command, but to swim. And there are other occasions when handlers use 'get over', such as when their dogs meet a hedge, when they want them just to go through the hedge.

There are also handlers who use the 'get over' command when the dog is at their side (in the sendaway position) to inform the dog that at some point in its outrun it will need to jump (or swim or in some way traverse) to get over an obstacle. So instead of using the command for the blind retrieve, the handler lines up the dog and says 'get over', pointing in the direction of the retrieve. The command, in this case, has now changed from meaning to jump, swim or traverse, to meaning 'you will be required to jump (swim or traverse) at some point later on, once you are travelling away'.

Something to consider here, when using this command to send the dog, is that, if you normally use differentiated sending for marks and blinds, by just saying 'get over', you are actually removing some of the information about the type of retrieve for the dog. Usually you are cueing 'a blind in that direction' or 'go and get that mark', but by using 'get over' instead you are just saying 'cross an obstacle at some point in that direction'.

Now, what happens when there are two obstacles en route to the retrieve? Does the handler need to say 'get over, get over', or does the dog know that the command means jump or traverse every obstacle in its path? And what if the handler doesn't know there is an obstacle to jump or negotiate, such as a hidden ditch or stream, or a fence out of sight down the hill or in a wood? Does the dog that hasn't been told to 'get over' just stop at the barrier and not carry on, because it has not been told to cross this obstacle? There appears to be a lot of ambiguity surrounding these scenarios. And if you are feeling slightly confused by what is meant at this point, then it is certain that many dogs are, too.

A dog that has been taught to jump correctly clears the wire fence with confidence without making contact with it. (Photo: John Jeffrey)

THE DOG'S EYE VIEW

Perhaps we first need to look at what the dog actually perceives to be a 'barrier'. I suspect that our own perception of what constitutes an obstacle may not be the same as the dog's. In Chapter 3 we looked at how dogs see the world differently to humans, and we should take this into account with their work in the field. For example, I set up a retrieve recently that was a long memory blind, where the dogs had to take a diagonal line through a natural 'corridor' of trees on the corner of a wood, then come out into open rough grassland, pass through a spinney of a few trees, and jump a stock fence into a paddock to the retrieve area (marked by a white stick).

If you asked each one of the handlers what the obstacle was in this scenario they would all have said the stock fence. However, this didn't appear to be the case for the dogs. As we sent each dog

in turn through the corridor of trees, they each ducked out of the row they were running in, pulling left to avoid a small tentacle of bramble and a patch of taller grass. This took them off the direct line of the retrieve. Each dog saw that small piece of vegetation as an obstacle, but not one of them saw the fence as any sort of barrier and jumped it without hesitation.

We need to look at the detail more, like a dog does. Think about a marked retrieve on mown grass over a wire fence, where the dog has a clear view of the dummy that has been thrown. How much of a barrier is that fence (for a dog that is familiar with jumping, and which has been taught to jump competently)? Now think about a marked retrieve for a dog where you are standing in longer grass and the dummy is thrown a distance out of the long grass on to shorter grass. How many dogs see the edge of the longer cover as a barrier and start to hunt there for the retrieve? Again, this can be solved with adequate training and familiarization.

But the point is, this is an obstruction for some dogs, and yet we sometimes fail to see these natural barriers ourselves. A change of terrain for a dog can be just as much a barrier as a physical obstacle such as a wall or a hedge, but I don't think I have ever heard a handler use 'get over' in these cases. Largely, we put our human interpretation on to what constitutes a legitimate barrier for the dog.

THE 'ONE COMMAND' OUTRUN

The way I approach work with barriers is not to put the idea of an obstacle into the dog's head in the first place. If 'go back' (or whatever your blind command is) means run in that direction and keep going until told otherwise, then the dog has all the information that it needs. It has been commanded to proceed in a particular direction, and understands that it should take on any changes of terrain that may be in its path, without detouring around them. There is no confusion as to whether it should run, jump or swim, or pass through a hedge or over two ditches. The instruction is to keep moving until it is told to stop or hunt.

I remember a complex retrieve that was set up for us as a group of handlers at a training ground recently. I lined my dog on his blind command to 'go back', and he left my side to run through the cover crop, jump a small wire fence, then cross a track and pass into some longer grass before dropping down a steep bank out of sight and into a pond. He then swam across the water to a long thin island in the pond, dropped down the other side of the island, re-entered the pond and swam to the far bank, where he crossed the long grass and track again. At this point I stopped him before he went out of sight to cross a steep-sided stream that he needed to negotiate before entering a wood on the hill where the retrieves were located. I put in the stop to 'recontact' him and just ensure that his line back into the obscured wooded area would be absolutely perfect. He picked quickly and came back via the same route. One of the other handlers then turned to me

and said: 'Gosh, "back" really does mean "back", doesn't it!'

With that in mind, I don't advocate continually pushing a dog with additional 'back' commands, because the dog should be working on the single command from the sendaway position. You wouldn't use two stop commands or three recall commands, or give repeated directions, so by the same token it shouldn't be necessary to reiterate the 'back' command repeatedly, if the dog has been taught to take and maintain that line. Some handlers do like to drive a dog onwards by shouting 'back', but this can end up being unnecessarily noisy if the distance is great, and it is quieter and cleaner to send the dog from heel and have it run without additional handler input directly to the desired area. You can strengthen this 'one command' outrun by doing plenty of memory blinds, where the dog is running confidently to an area, and gradually increasing the distance.

If you get to the point where the dog is slowing down or stopping and looking for input, rather than pushing the dog onwards again with additional 'back' commands, bring the dog back and reset the exercise to ensure success (by re-marking the area so the dog is confident there is something there, or shortening the distance before rebuilding again). Rather than pushing the dog when he starts to flag with an extra 'back', so that he starts to rely on this extra support as he goes out to a certain distance, instead consider supporting his strong outrun with praise, so he learns that running out hard is rewarding. You will eventually drop this praise once he has learned the concept.

If you can do away with some of your extraneous commands, then much of your handling will be to maintain a watching brief, being ready to respond if something goes wrong, or if the dog needs additional help and input to complete the retrieve. The Kennel Club Field Trial Regulations, J(A)3.1. actually states: 'Noisy handling, however er occasioned, is a major fault. A good handler will appear to do little but watch his dog while maintaining at all times perfect control over it.' This brings to mind a quote from *The Karate Kid* (2010), where Mr Han says to his young charge: 'There's a big difference between stillness and

Walls and water are some of the 'barriers' that your dog
may encounter on the way to a retrieve.

Build your line work positively so that you can send the dog with a single command from your side and it will keep going despite any changes in terrain.

doing nothing.' Much of the art of successful retriever handling is observing and being ready to act quickly if necessary.

DEALING WITH A STRONG WIND

One of the biggest 'barriers' for a dog can be dealing with a strong wind. The majority of dogs do not enjoy running into a wind or being handled into it, just as we wouldn't enjoy jogging or cycling into it! It isn't a pleasant feeling. It is far easier to run with the wind on your back and your face away from it.

Invariably when you send a dog out on a retrieve with a strong crosswind, he will sink or drift on it so that he ends up a fair way downwind of where you were initially aiming. If scenting conditions are good, you may be lucky in that he catches wind of the retrieve if he hasn't drifted too far. But if he is substantially off course once he has made the distance, you will have quite a fight to try and cast him directly into the wind to get

him back on the line. You may find he refuses to cast and face the wind, and repeatedly pulls back, rather than taking the left- or right-handed cast. With this in mind, think strategically when you line up the dog for such a retrieve. Aim further upwind of where you would ideally want the dog to end up. If he sinks the wind, this will bring him directly on course for the retrieve, or within scenting distance. And if he doesn't sink the wind, you will have an easy stop and cast with the wind to bring him into the area.

In less extreme conditions, use the wind to your advantage. For example, when lining on a memory mark, don't make your line so accurate that the dog reaches the area directly, but maybe very slightly upwind. Err to the downwind side when you line, so that the dog has the benefit of scent when he reaches the area. He will have his memory of the depth to help him too, if he's been taught to mark accurately, but keeping the wind in mind will ensure success.

133

At all times, it is vital to know what the wind is doing. Use it to your advantage when you practise handling. Think carefully about when to handle in relation to the wind. Give the dog an opportunity to pick for itself when it is in or near the area of the retrieve, but once it is safely out of the area where the wind would enable it to scent the retrieve, then step in to handle the dog. This means the dog is less likely to override your commands, with no scent stimulus.

AVOIDING THE BUNKERS

When you look at a complex retrieve, it is useful to think of it in terms of playing a hole on a golf course. From the point that you send the dog, you can look out to the area of the retrieve and can decide what par it is – how many casts/commands ideally it should take you to pick the dummy or bird. You will need to think about what constitutes the 'fairway', where the bunkers are (and how you can stay out of them), and what in the terrain might pull the dog off course, preventing you from reaching the putting green. The bunkers are factors in the terrain that might hinder the dog from getting from A to B, or more importantly, hinder your visibility of it. They are where you do not want to be.

It is tempting to fixate on the area of the retrieve, the 'putting green'. But it is far more important to think, instead, about what the barriers are in getting to that area efficiently. As well as obvious physical barriers such as woodland, a stream, wall or ditch, there may be an unusual camber to the ground that takes a dog off course, or a strong wind to deal with. Additional factors that would influence the dog might include pulling towards the shot/gun rather than the fall, a dummy thrower, previous falls or retrieve areas, game scent or live game. In addition, difficult cover or expanses of water may push a dog off its line. As a handler, you will need to take these elements into account, both when you plan the retrieve and as the retrieve progresses. It is the handler's job to keep the dog away from bunkers and in the central 'corridor' for the retrieve.

KEEPING IN CONTACT WITH YOUR DOG

It is not just the dog that can get in a bunker and disappear from sight. Sometimes we need to think about what the dog can see when it looks back at us. On occasions handlers unwittingly obscure themselves from the dog: if the dog is working in tall cover, remember to keep your arm signals for casting and for directional hunting much higher, so that the dog can see them. In addition, if you are standing in tall cover yourself, the dog will look back and only see the top half of your torso, which gives it a very unfamiliar picture of you, if it is accustomed to seeing you out training in a plain grass field, where your legs are usually visible. This can confuse a young dog, as its visual picture will be dramatically altered.

Also, if you are walking up in a long gun line, and you need to handle your dog when it is down the line, remember to step well out of the line, not only so your dog can pick you out, but so that your hand signals are not hidden by the other people in the line. It is sometimes enlightening to be out in the field throwing dummies and to look back at the sea of handlers from the dog's position, so you see what the dog sees (albeit from a more elevated level). It is often extremely difficult to see hand signals, particularly against a drab background of trees or hedges, or with the sun in the wrong position.

As well as staying in visual contact with your dog, another consideration is remaining in aural contact. Again, wind direction can make all the difference here. If the dog is running downwind from you he is far more likely to hear the whistle clearly than if he is upwind. You can test this with a friend out in the field at distance, to see how the sound of the whistle is affected between you.

Terrain will also affect how well sound carries, in particular working in a dense root crop as opposed to working on arable land or moorland. When a dog runs out in grassland it can usually hear the whistle very well, depending on wind direction. However, the dog running through sugar beet will have to contend with the noise of the crunching leaves as it breaks through them.

It isn't enough to rely on *hearing* – the dog needs to be trained to run out actively *listening*

It is often difficult for a dog to pick out its handler from the line, particularly against a dark background.

for its next command. This is a new challenge for many. And handlers often get a shock when they work their dogs in root crops for the first time, and find that their previously whistle-perfect dog has gone temporarily deaf, or has developed what some have termed 'sugar-beet-itis' (characterized by wild running)!

WORKING TOWARDS TIGHTER LINES

As your dog gets more proficient and you start working to a higher standard (particularly for those competing, and looking at Open level competitions) there will come a time when you will need to make your retrieves more precise. When the dog is confident at running out strongly on a blind or memory at a distance of around eighty yards, you should think about being more critical about the line it takes to that area.

In your early build-up work on blinds, you may have 'seeded' the retrieve area with several dummies spread out to ensure success, so that once the dog had made the distance of the retrieve it would pick easily as a reward. This will have improved momentum and confidence. It is now time to think about asking for greater accuracy in that initial line.

One of the ways that you can do this is to build back from a target area (or using a visual white dummy), gradually incorporating more obstacles together with increasing the distance. For example, on the retrieve that I set up above, we started by throwing several dummies around a white stick that was twenty yards back from a stock fence. We walked from that area, taking the dogs over the fence as we climbed over ourselves, on a diagonal line, which passed through a small spinney and out into some rough grass. At

Dogs have to get used to running and working in 'noisy' root crops, such as sugar beet, where they will find it hard to hear whistle commands.

this point we turned round and sent the dogs on the line we had come, requiring them to take the direct line through the spinney and negotiating the fence on the diagonal.

Once the dogs were competent with this, we then continued to walk the line back the same distance again, leaving the grass area and moving halfway into the wood. We repeated the sends from this position, before moving back once more, this time progressing through the corner of the wood and out on to a mowed grass ride the other side. From this final position, the dogs would have the easier option to run around the wood, avoiding the cover, or they could take the direct line, which is what we wanted. Because we had 'walked the line' we had built the retrieve in a positive way, so the dogs had confidence in what they were doing, even though in places it was the more challenging option.

You can use features in the ground to make a point about holding a line, sometimes building the blind retrieve backwards in the manner described above, sometimes by using marks as an incentive to take the direct line, and sometimes by 'testing' the dog by setting up the full blind retrieve to see what it does, and then feeding back to it accordingly and repairing the parts that went wrong. Look for short, technical retrieves that will provide a test of the concept: for example, across a track that bears round to the right, but you want your dog to hold a straight line to twelve o'clock into longer grass; or through a patch of bracken directly in line with the retrieve, where the dog could choose to run round it rather than going straight to the retrieve. The use of these features will help you build in the concept of taking a direct line, rather than picking the most comfortable or the easiest path.

The same precision should be applied to the return from the retrieve as well as to the outrun. Sometimes the draw of a marked retrieve is enough to pull a dog out through some awkward cover, or across water, but once he has picked the retrieve he then opts to run round the obstacle, taking an easier path to return. If a dog has gone out one way, directly, there is usually no reason why it cannot come back via the same route – other than it is now focusing on any uncertainty about the terrain it is encountering. This detouring on the return shows a weakness in recall, and it is worth revisiting this basic obedience element in a wider variety of cover and incorporating more obstacles, to strengthen this return through cover.

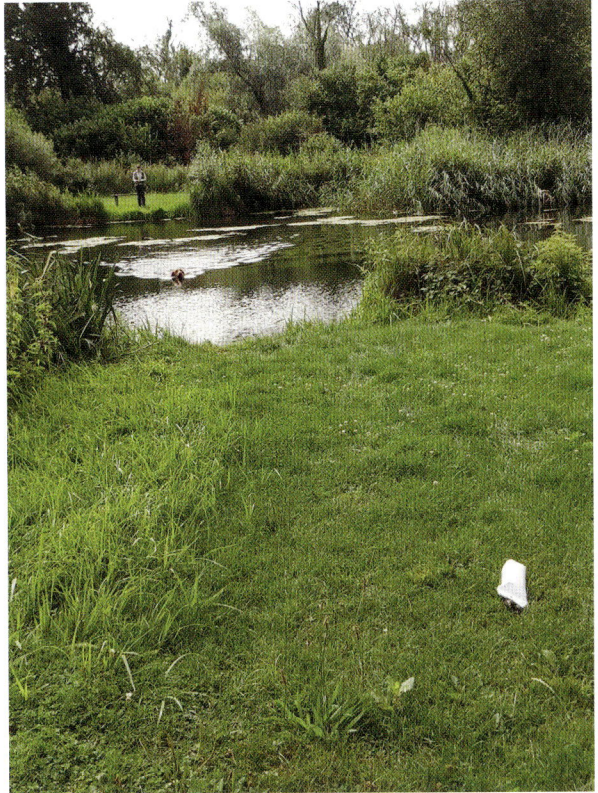

Building a retrieve back from a target area to incorporate changes in terrain and increase distance in increments.

11 THE DEVIL IS IN THE DETAIL

The detail is as important as the essential is. When it is inadequate, it destroys the whole outfit.

Christian Dior, fashion designer

Whilst we refrained from insisting on complete accuracy on some of the young dog's early out-run work (in order to preserve momentum and confidence), there are certain areas where you should not accept compromise, and these should be revisited to ensure quality is maintained.

To look at some of this detail, it is invaluable to spend time watching not only your own dog and those of others, but also other handlers too: what they do and how the dogs relate to them and their actions. Then take a look at yourself when you are handling. You will need somebody to video you to do this, but it's a useful exercise. Take a step back, be perceptive, and notice the small things that you might normally gloss over when you are working the dog yourself. You can learn so much through observation. Sometimes we do things, through habit, without knowing we do them. Cast a critical eye over both your own behaviour and that of your dog. This is where the benefit of having a private trainer or mentor comes in: he or she can focus on the minutiae of what you are actually doing, spot issues as they arise, and give you strategies to change your handling, and nip any bad habits in the bud.

ATTITUDE AT HEEL

As we discussed in Chapter 6, good heelwork is critical, and informs so much more than just being able to walk comfortably with a dog at your side. It affects the whole sendaway set-up, not only with regard to accuracy of line, but also in terms of attitude to the retrieve.

Take care to notice how the dog is relating to you and the retrieve when he is at heel. Locking on to the retrieve is desirable, but over-investment in it at the expense of steadiness is another thing altogether. Do not allow the retrieve to take over in the dog's head. Set up exercises where the young dog will lock on to the mark, and be given it as a reward in some cases, but in others require the dog to 'lock off' by turning away at heel with you and walking in the opposite direction.

Do not reward pushy behaviour – prancing, paddling of the front legs, lungeing or excessive panting – with any retrieve. Wait until the dog exhibits calm behaviour before you send it. A sensible attitude at heel is key to a reliable partnership.

As you progress through your training, also be on the lookout for any signs of anticipation in the dog, and stay one step ahead of him in your training, being ready to adapt what you were going to do, so that the dog has to take all his direction from you, rather than second-guessing what you might be about to do.

CARRIAGE AND DELIVERY

Like many of the elements of rudimentary training, it is easier to get carriage and delivery of the retrieve ingrained from an early age, so that it becomes a good habit (we looked at early 'hold' conditioning in Chapter 5). But sometimes this needs revisiting in the later stages of training as the work becomes more exciting or demanding.

CARRIAGE IN THE RETRIEVE

A poor hold can stem from a difficult pick up, from speed – the dog is going too fast when he picks – unfamiliarity of the retrieve item, or over-tiredness or over-heating of the dog. Look out for sloppy holds on the dummy as the dog returns with the retrieve, and be consistent in gently re-seating the dummy in the dog's mouth if it doesn't have a central hold. You don't need to make a big issue about it, but taking care in this respect will pay dividends with the transition on to game, where the dog needs to hold the bird by the body to maintain a good grip, rather than picking and carrying it by the head, a leg or the tail.

Another thing to look out for on the return is the dog paying too much attention to the retrieve in his mouth, and starting to play with it. This can be manifested either in the dog rolling or mouthing the dummy, or in extreme cases starting to fling it about or chew on it. This is not a 'mouth' issue, but usually rather a recall and focus issue. The dog has made the retrieve, but has switched from the desired routine of filling its mouth and

returning, with its primary focus on getting back to its handler, to, instead, starting to think more about the pleasure of the article in its mouth. This has now outweighed the importance of the handler. Sometimes the excitement of the outrun or a prolonged hunt can stimulate this behaviour on the return.

If you start to notice that the dog is doing this, then it is advisable to go back to recall work to rectify it. Focus on ensuring a strong recall (without the retrieve), and then gradually reintroduce the retrieve by back-chaining the previous elements – that is, recalling the dog towards the dummy to pick it, and back in to the handler. Once this remedial work is done, reintroduce the outrun and the 'full' retrieve again.

Mouthing on return may also result from perceived pressure by the dog. If he is anxious because he has done something wrong, or he has been reprimanded for some reason, he may

Returning with a good central hold of the dummy.

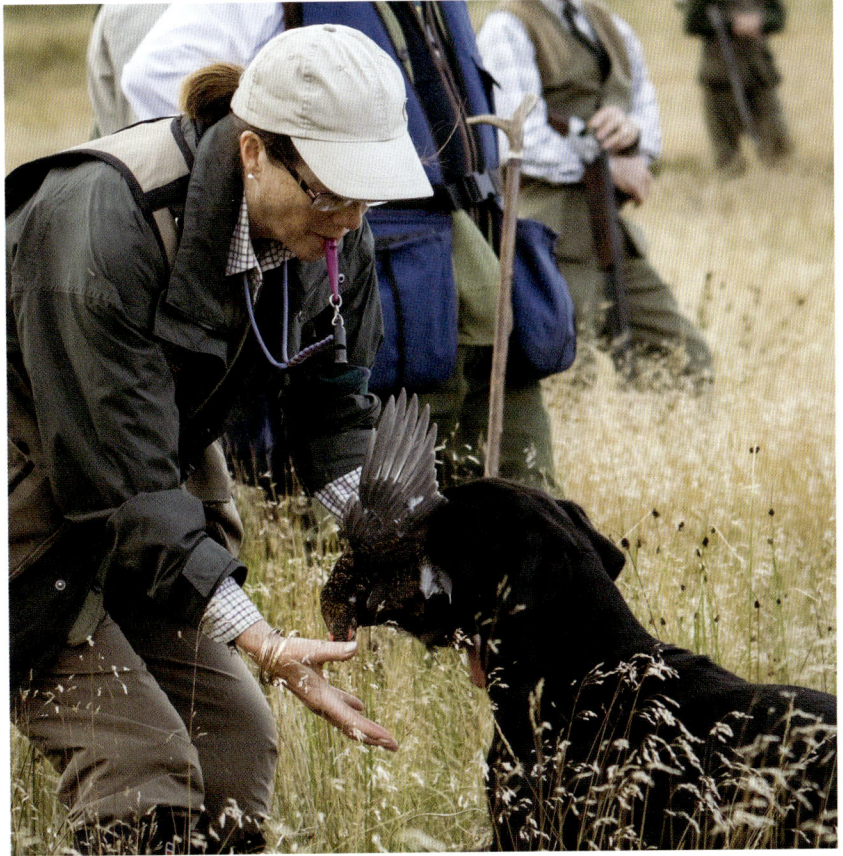

Delivery should be tenderly to hand, with the retrieve released on command, rather than being dragged out of the dog's mouth. (Photo: Caroline Dell)

transfer this anxiety and start to roll or bite down on the dummy. If you have created some pressure or negativity, try to lift this from the dog and balance it with praise when the dog is doing something right. Sometimes for a sensitive dog pressure can accumulate, and handlers don't notice the build-up and the negative impact it is having.

It is very important to keep any corrections short and 'in the moment', rather than bearing grudges, and also to ensure that any pressure that they might create is lifted straightaway afterwards by rewarding good behaviour, so that the dog can return to the status quo. In some cases, just returning to the line, where there may be several people, can cause a young and inexperienced dog to feel pressure. Be vigilant in watching for any signs of concern in your dog as he returns to you, and do what you can to relieve this by making his return fun, with praise or a thrown tennis ball after he has delivered.

THE DELIVERY TO HAND

As well as how the dog carries the retrieve, look at the point of release: the delivery to hand. Take care to be sure what the dog understands as his command to release the retrieve into your hand. What is the cue to drop? Is it your hand coming towards him, or moving under his chin? Are you moving forwards or bending over him, which

also causes him to drop? You can check this, and if so, rectify it.

Think about delivery in terms of the dog bringing the retrieve and 'giving' it to you, rather than you 'taking' it away from him. Try putting your hands behind your back as the dog comes in, to prevent you from grabbing or lungeing for the dummy. You want to encourage the dog to offer up or give you the retrieve, almost to the point that he is forcing it upon you, and sharing it with you, rather than you confiscating it. You don't want the dog to let go of the retrieve until he is commanded to release it with a cue word such as 'dead'.

A sloppy delivery will be exacerbated when the dog comes out of water, when it will be tempted to shake, to relieve its coat of water, and may drop or abandon the retrieve in the process. Needless to say, this is an eliminating fault in competition, and highly undesirable in the field, as the wound-

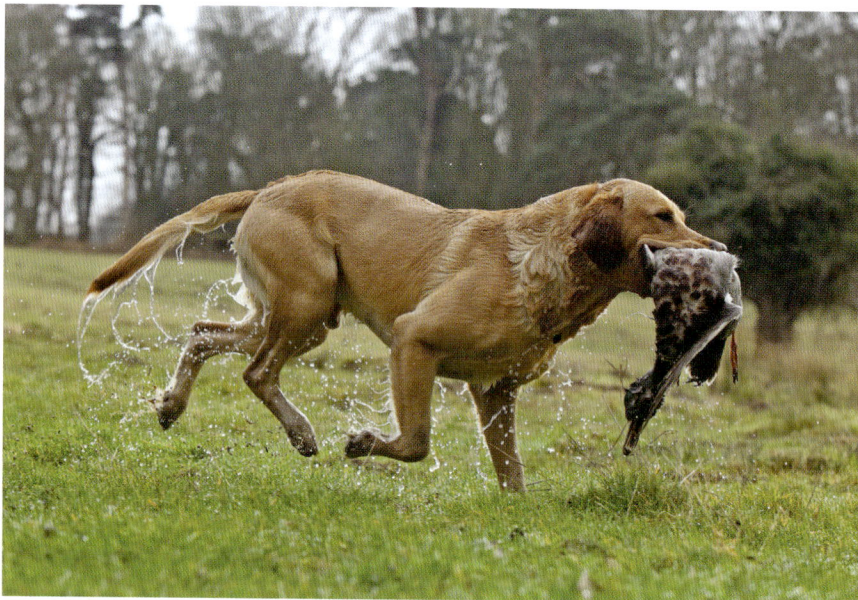

A fast return out of water without shaking is ideal.

ed game may escape from the dog if dropped. If your dog is a persistent dropper out of water, look again at its attitude to deliveries on land, before trying to rectify the situation out of water. You may find that the fundamental mechanics are not in place soundly from the start.

After the dog has delivered out of water, use a 'shake' command to encourage it to shake itself to remove the excess water from its coat. By doing this, you are letting the dog know when it is acceptable to shake, and when it is not.

DIRECTIONAL BACKS

Once the young dog understands the concept of the 'back' command from a remote position in the field (the dog starts facing you, then turns round 180 degrees and runs away), then you can

Shaking after delivery on command.

start to insist that it turns on the correct shoulder according to which hand you use to push the dog back.

Most handlers are right-handed, and consequently use their right arm as the signal to push the dog back. This usually means that the dog will turn on its left shoulder (anti-clockwise) to go back. This becomes a habit, and the dog will begin to favour this side for turning after a while, just as, given the choice, right-handed people prefer to use the right arm for the push back. You can test how one-sided your dog is by giving it a 'back' command with the left arm signal (if you are right-handed), and notice which way it turns. If it continues to turn on its left shoulder (to your right) then you know that it has ingrained this habit, or it has greater strength on this side.

It may seem very picky to insist on the dog turning on the appropriate shoulder (relating to the arm signal) when you command it back. But far from being a 'circus trick', this skill is very useful in the field. For example, if the dog is likely to 'slip the wind' (if there is a strong cross wind) as we discussed in the previous chapter, and end up drifting too far away, then it is sensible to turn the dog into the wind on the back cast, which will help you to get a squarer cast back. If you turn him downwind, it is more likely the wind will continue to push him further that way.

To teach your dog to turn on the 'correct' shoulder, you can set him up for success by leaving him remotely in the field quarter-turned towards the direction of travel. So, if you are casting him with the left arm, have him facing directly left (rather than facing you squarely).

This means it is easier for him only to have to make a 90-degree turn to complete the back cast on the correct shoulder. To make the cast incorrectly, he would have to pivot around a full 270 degrees. The chances for success are greatly increased using this method.

When you have practised this several times on both shoulders, and the dog understands the concept, you can add a side dummy into the equation. The first time you do this, use the side dummy to cement the idea of the directional 'back' cast being different to a cast either left or right. So, if you are pushing back on your left hand then you will put the other dummy out to the right-hand side of the dog. The dog will see the clear differentiation of pushing back with the left hand as being fundamentally different to casting right for the other dummy, as it is the opposite hand.

This exercise is useful, as it directly translates to a scenario whereby you have been asked to pick a bird that is further back from the dog, but you are aware that there are other birds out to the side in the field that he may wind if you push him back with that hand. To ensure success of picking the correct bird, you would push him back on the opposing hand.

To test that the dog has truly grasped the concept of always turning on the correct shoulder,

The dog placed facing left, ready to push back left-handed, turning on its right shoulder.

you can then set up the exercise in reverse of the methods described above. So you change the angle of where the dog is facing on his remote stand/sit in the field, whereby he is not angled in favour of the cast, but is actually angled away from it. This means he will have to make a very concerted effort to turn on the correct shoulder. And finally, you can use the second dummy placed out for a left/right cast, but put it to the same side that you are requiring your 'back' cast on. That means, if you are pushing back left, then the other dummy would also be put out to the dog's left. The dog must now listen carefully for the 'back' command (rather than a left cast command) and watch for the 'back' hand signal, as opposed to the casting left arm signal. It is worth trying this exercise periodically to keep your casting accurate, and to ensure that the back command has not become sloppy.

FINE TUNING YOUR TRAINING

MAINTAIN A BALANCED RELATIONSHIP

A keen retriever makes training much more enjoyable than one that is reluctant or less motivated on dummies. If the dog has 'plenty in the tank' it means that multiple call-backs for taking a wrong line, or repeated training drills, are more readily tolerated, than in a dog with less drive. But there is a line to be drawn between keenness and letting the retrieve take over in the dog's head. The dog should remain level and balanced, in partnership with you, without letting the excitement of the retrieve take over and without any pre-empting.

Periodically it is worth reviewing this balance and ensuring that the dog sees you as the centre of the retrieving equation. An exercise you can do to check this relationship, is to sit up the dog remotely, facing you. Throw a dummy behind it and then walk away some forty metres and turn and face the dog again. Next, recall the dog to front. If the dog is properly trained on the recall, it will come straight back to you, ignoring the distraction of the dummy behind it.

But what happens next is critical, and the part that you should be most interested in. It should 'present' to you at front, facing you, as it would have been taught as a puppy, giving you full attention. However, many dogs will recall on the whistle, but once they arrive in the vicinity of their handler, will spin round and put themselves straight on to the handler's heel, facing the direction of the retrieve, giving this priority. I call this 'self-setting'. The dog is so keen to get to the retrieve that it has by-passed the handler in the equation, and is getting itself into the 'go' position. At this point, the handler has become secondary in the dog's mind. The canvas dummy has taken over and become more important and overriding. Many handlers don't notice this, others just say that their dog is keen, and still others say 'I didn't teach him to do that. He just does it!'.

It is important to pay attention to this. Although it is a small detail, it is something that reflects the

Look again at the recall and the way the dog presents to front. The dog should be focused on you when it returns.

After recalling the dog to front, leave it where it is and step round to its side, rather than letting it finish to heel.

nature of your partnership with the dog. You do want your dog to remain keen to retrieve, but he should also understand that access to that reward comes from you, and is available on your terms rather than on his. When he gives you eye contact and respect, then you can reward this with the retrieve. The more he pulls to face towards the retrieve, the more you should back away, and re-request him to recall to front facing you. In this way, he will be getting further and further away from the retrieve, until he exhibits the behaviour that you have requested.

Where 'self-setting' has become an ingrained habit in a dog, it is also an idea to temporarily remove the finish to heel after you have got the recall to front successfully. These two behaviours – present to front/delivery and then finish to heel – are joined together quickly as a habit after a successful retrieve. But for the purposes of re-setting the equation, it is worth removing the finish to heel, and instead leave the dog sitting where he has presented, then you step round to the dog's side. This just takes the 'habit' away for a while and gets the dog to stay sitting where he has presented (facing towards you and away from the retrieve area).

RIGHT ON THE FIRST ATTEMPT

When you are training, it is often necessary to repeat an exercise, sometimes several times, in order for the dog to get it right. This may involve calling the dog back to try again, or at other times repeatedly handling the dog. When the dog is in the early stages of schooling, this is an accepted part of training. The dog will learn how to go right by sometimes going wrong, and if it is not fully competent or fluent in the behaviours, there will be a greater propensity for errors. Working through these mistakes will also help the young dog develop its resilience.

However, there will come a time in the advanced stages of training where you decide that the dog should not be offered a second chance on certain retrieves, as it is starting to get into a pattern of being recalled, then redoing the exercise and getting it right the second time. Sometimes a dog will not apply itself diligently on a first attempt, but when re-sent, will get it right. Obviously this is not a pattern that is going to be acceptable for a dog that is competing, where it will only get one chance to make the retrieve.

In this case, it is worth adopting a system of 'denials' if you are repeatedly not getting the behaviour that you want on the first attempt. For example, if a dog goes out to the fall on a mark and starts to hunt but straightaway 'explodes' out of the area, bring it in without picking and let it sit out for a turn or two before you re-try it. The dog is not really concentrating fully on the job in hand, and has lost focus. It hasn't made an intelligent effort in the area, and there is no value in letting it find the retrieve by brawn alone, or by chance. There is also no value in sending it straight back, as it will learn that it will just get a second attempt if it doesn't apply itself properly the first time. Denying the dog the retrieve often has the effect of making the dog try harder on subsequent retrieves. It focuses its mind.

When you consider denials, do not be afraid of bringing a dog in empty-mouthed, either. One of the necessary skills, both for trialling and for picking up when trying for a bird that the gun believes may have been pricked, is being able to call the dog back without it having picked any-thing. Some dogs are reluctant to return with-out filling their mouths. For trialling, you may be tried on several 'dry runs' where the bird is not found, going behind other dogs to hunt a given area. The dog will need to operate under control, hunt the designated area, and then be ready to be called in after it has made its search, if noth-ing is found. Repeated recalling of a dog that is failing to come back without a bird will see your speedy exit from a trial, or will prove embarrass-ing, at least, on a shoot.

AURAL-ONLY COMMANDS

A further detail to consider, when you are fine-tuning your handling, is that of vocal- or aural-only commands to the dog. By this we mean cut-ting out accompanying body language, which may be cueing the dog in preference to the sound signal. For example, when you recall a young dog you will often blow the recall whis-tle in conjunction with using open, outstretched arms. This forms a very powerful visual stimulus, in addition to the whistle tone, to draw the dog to come towards you. As the dog becomes more familiar with the recall command, then it is worth working on omitting the arm signal so that you can be certain that the dog is recalling on the whistle tone alone, whether it can see you or not. This will be especially necessary when the dog is

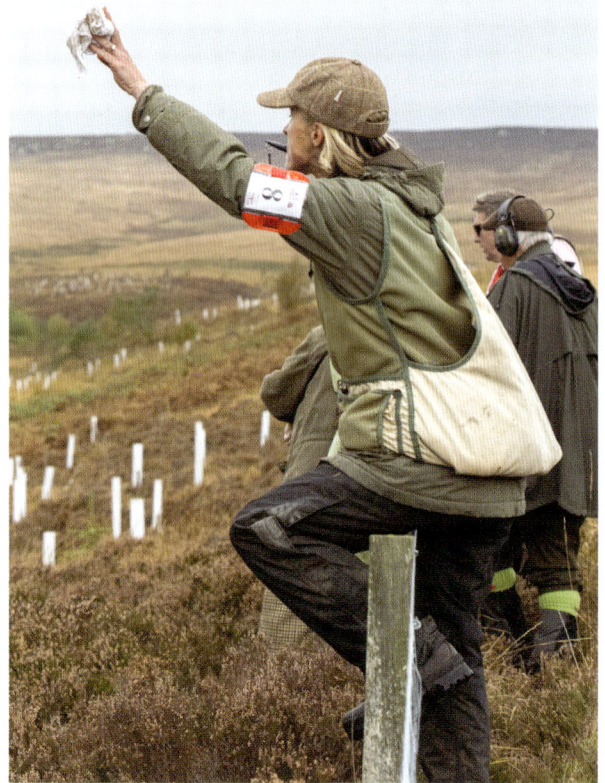

Give yourself every advantage if the dog is working in difficult terrain by getting on to some higher ground or a vantage point from where you may be able to see to handle. (Photo: Mollie Lord Photography)

working in a wood or tall cover.

Next you might want to consider your stop whistle. Arguably this is an 'aural-only' command anyway, as the dog is usually running away from you when you blow it, so there is no immediate visual stimulus. But quite often, other factors do anchor the stop whistle, such as the picture that the dog sees when he turns in response to the whistle to orientate towards his handler. He will be used to seeing you with your hand up to 'hold' him in the stop. Practise stops without this visual signal, as well as practising with it and then dropping the hand down, to ensure that the dog doesn't move off as soon as the body-language picture changes.

Another way of testing how established your stop whistle actually is, is by blowing it as you are walking with the dog at heel. If you can do this as you walk, and the dog drops on the whistle whilst you continue walking without breaking your stride, and without any arm signals (or body 'tells'), then it is likely that your stop whistle is fully conditioned. The dog has overridden the visual stimulus of you still moving on, with the aural command that it has received for 'stop'. Also, practise out of sight remote stops, behind a hedge or wall, with the aid of a friend to report whether the dog is still stopping. You want to know that the stop whistle still works when you are fully or partially obscured.

Finally, consider no-handed directional commands, which can be useful for handling a dog when it can't see you. 'Back' is relatively easy to achieve with no arm signal, but directions left and right are much harder to achieve, as this will require the dog to discriminate with no visual support. Weigh up whether it is worth the extra time to try and achieve no-handed left and right. It is something that I tried (see Chapter 3) but do not feel that I ever attained consistently.

It is worth remembering here, that when the dog is out of sight to us, we are not always out of sight to him. For example, in a cover crop you may not be able to see the dog as you look down on the crop, but quite often the dog can still see you from where it is sitting, or at least the top half of you. So continue to use your arm signals to support the vocal command, even if you think the dog won't see much of it. It may just catch enough movement to reinforce the cast correctly.

12 A WINNING COMBINATION

What does it take to be a champion? Desire, dedication, determination, concentration and the will to win.

Patty Berg, American athlete

While many readers will be looking to improve their performance in working tests and field trials, for others this isn't the ultimate aim. The journey of growing the partnership with your dog and improving its training is just as fulfilling. If success in competitions is important to you, however, then your approach, attitude and frame of mind will determine whether you succeed or fail. In addition to an effective training programme, developing strength of mind is a really important part of being able to compete at the higher levels, and it is this that will eventually prevail over any sort of innate ability on the part of the handler.

Becoming a 'champion trainer' takes tenacity. It means keeping going when the going gets tough, and accepting that there will be a certain amount of stress and pressure along the way. You will need to prepare for it, both mentally and physically. Trialling is demanding in terms of effort, resources, time, money and demands on your home life and character. Once the shooting season starts, retriever trials are packed into a relatively short period of a couple of months before the Retriever Championship at the beginning of December, and it can feel very much like an endurance test to keep going in a bid to qualify for this prestigious event. The two day Open stakes (where a win qualifies you for the Championship) are a real test of a dog and handler, to maintain their composure and consistency over that full period, without a single slip-up.

Some people will say that performance at trials is mostly down to luck on the day. It is true that fortune does definitely have a role to play in what is shot, and how, during the trial, and whose retrieve it is next. These are things over which you can have no bearing. You can't control the presentation of birds or game, but your training will effectively prepare you for how to deal with the retrieves you are offered. This preparation is paramount. If you and your dog are ready for every likely scenario, then this will improve your confidence, as you know that you can deal with most situations.

There are other things that are within your control, including your own nerves or anxiety. Being in control of your mind will mean that you perform more consistently under pressure, and that you will find the experience more enjoyable, and in turn will increase your chance of success.

Unlike in most competitive sports, you are not pitted against other players: instead it is you and your dog against the retrieve that has been allocated. In this respect, mental stamina is very important, as well as maintaining your focus and not becoming distracted. It isn't just about being better than the others. Whereas in a game of tennis or golf, if others don't perform well and you do better, you will win – but this is not so in trialling. You have to be up to the standard required, performing at the highest level to achieve the win. If you aren't good enough, the win or place may be withheld.

Even the best dog and handler partnership won't win everything. But you can aim to keep trying to be better. Training for competition is a great way to incentivize your training and spur you on to continue making improvements. Think about what you want to achieve, what is realistic, and set long- and short-term goals to help you accomplish this, whilst also keeping an eye on the training process.

Working on the moor tests the stamina of both dog and handler. (Photo: Caroline Dell)

HAVE A GAME PLAN

As with day-to-day training, when you compete, you need to have a plan in place. If you are working with a trainer or mentor, they should help you with your preparation for competition, and be very much more than somebody who just throws dummies for you. The best ones will guide you, when the time is right, to think about competing and everything that is involved with that. They will help you get to grips with the Kennel Club J Regulations governing field trials, as well as the procedures and formats that you can expect in tests and trials. They will have the sort of 'inside information' and knowledge that comes from years of participation. They should also encourage you to help or at least spectate at a few events, before actually participating, so that you know what to expect.

THREAT AND ERROR MANAGEMENT

I recently came across an approach used in the airline industry that has relevance to retriever competition work, in particular working tests, which are more formulaic than field trials. Psychologists at the University of Texas designed the Threat and Error Management (TEM) model, in 1994, from analysing airline incidents and accidents. This framework helps pilots to manage in-flight challenges effectively, detecting and responding to events as well as managing mistakes and risks that may occur during a flight, to maintain safety. It puts threats and errors into specific contexts, enabling performance planning to be appropriate, and incorporates technical as well as environmental issues. It also encourages mindfulness, to help prevent undesired outcomes.

The same principles could be applied to competitive retrieve scenarios, in the context of managing challenges that might arise during competition, here similarly identified as threats and errors.

Threats: Events and circumstances that are beyond the influence of the handler, and which fall into three categories:

• Anticipated: weather conditions, bunkers, terrain, previous falls.

Competing requires both mental and physical stamina, but is a rewarding way of seeing the fruits of your labour. (Photo: Caroline Dell)

- Unanticipated: unseen obstacles, optical illusions, spectator interference.
- Latent: handler fatigue, confidence, lack of proficiency/experience.

Errors: Actions (or inaction) by the handler:

- Slips/lapses: forgetting where the mark is, casting the dog incorrectly.
- Rule-based mistakes: sending the dog before the judge has told you.
- Knowledge-based mistakes: hunting the dog in the wrong area.

To deal with these, the handler should have a reaction strategy in place, which might be categorized in three stages: anticipate, recognize and recover.

Anticipate: When given the retrieve scenario, assess the wind direction and strength, look for any obvious bunkers, and be aware of where the guns/throwers are in relation to the retrieve. Are there any factors that will provide 'suction' for the dog, such as previous falls or terrain that will make them drop away from the retrieve area? Knowing your own dog's strengths and weaknesses is important here. Have a plan in place for how you will tackle the retrieve.

Recognize: Once the dog is sent for the retrieve, monitor its progress carefully and be ready to react if it starts to go off course. You will see if it is sinking the wind or being drawn towards a bunker, or another retrieve.

Recover: Assess the situation quickly and make timely decisions to correct the dog's course, before it is too late to recover from any bunkers. Intervene with appropriate handling to put the dog in the right place to find the retrieve.

Waiting in the gallery at a trial, there is time to consider the wind, terrain and scenting conditions, and how these will affect retrieves. (Photo: Caroline Dell)

PROGRESSING TO A PROFESSIONAL LEVEL

There may come a point when your hobby has become more of a lifestyle and you feel you want to engage in the sport in a more professional way, not necessarily as a trainer yourself but participating and competing at higher levels. Moving from novice or amateur status up through the ranks brings with it additional pressure, whether that is self-imposed, with a desire to achieve results for yourself or for sponsors, or from the expectations of peers and rivals. You will need to push out of your comfort zone, and be prepared for additional scrutiny.

Pressure to continue succeeding on a more public platform can be daunting at times. However, the natural cycle of gundog training, from puppyhood through novice to open level, means that you will be able to dip back into these less serious tests when you have younger dogs coming through behind your older, more experienced dogs. It is refreshing to bring on a new and promising young novice dog, or to start off a puppy in the basics, whilst still ticking over an open level or advanced dog.

Once you have developed your own style and methods, and you have had more dogs through your hands, you will find that your training becomes increasingly efficient and streamlined. But it is always worth being receptive to trying new teaching methods to see how they work with different dogs.

KEY POINTS FOR 'CHAMPION TRAINERS'

- Trust your ability as a trainer
- Retain motivation levels by setting achievable short-term goals
- Develop mental fortitude: deal with pressure
- Avoid complacency: seek out new ideas and techniques
- Be perceptive
- Work on timing; feedback to the dog

PERFECTION: THE HOLY GRAIL?

Just as there are no flawless human beings, there is no such thing as a 'perfect dog'. There are no perfect dogs in any of the UK's top kennels, but there are some extremely good ones that competent trainers have been able to work with to make champions in the field. But alongside these dogs' strengths lie their own foibles and weaknesses.

Build a strong bond with your dog, and that partnership of love and trust will take you anywhere.

dog. Yes, I replied. He said 'Oh, I didn't think you would keep her'! He thought her lack of drive in that situation was an innate trait, and he perhaps thought that it couldn't be addressed. To me, the behaviour that she exhibited on that particular occasion wasn't an issue, but I knew we had some work to do on improving confidence in large groups and preparation for this sort of moorland terrain. We addressed this weakness, which was primarily due to her lack of exposure.

Another young dog, early on in her training, would avoid facing cover if she could find an easier path. Again, this is not an uncommon trait in an inexperienced dog. We worked on this by building our line work backwards from pieces of cover or off-putting terrain. Once she understood the concept, and was trained methodically, she actively began to drive towards cover without hesitation.

Our aim is to work on these areas of weakness, to try to improve on them as much as possible. That is where the majority of our training is directed. And then, as the Johnny Mercer (1945) song says, we 'accentuate the positive' for the rest.

Some years ago I took a young dog for its first time out in a large group to another trainer on an unfamiliar ground. The young bitch ran a bit 'flat' but completed the retrieves. Three months later, I took her back and she flew across the course. The trainer asked me if it was the same

IMPROVING PERFORMANCE AS A TEAM

Retriever training is not a complicated process, if you have the right starting material provided with good breeding. To get the very best out of your partnership with your dog, you will need to build a strong bond so that the dog trusts and believes you, when he has to rely on you. In turn, you will have to trust his innate natural abilities when he is working on scent. This is a symbiotic relationship that at its very best will be seamless and enduring.

Advanced retriever work is a continuation of basic processes (including obedience and handling), with more attention paid to some of the 'detail' that is easy to gloss over, or which may be less interesting or exciting. It isn't just about making the retrieving distances longer or doing more control work instead of marks – it is about noticing the detail as well as the big picture, and working out ways to gradually improve your overall performance as a team.

No book will provide you with all the 'answers', but if *Advanced Retriever Training* has empowered you to think about your training and look at your canine-human partnership in a fresh, inspired way, then it has done its job. Appraising yourself honestly, as well as your dog, and asking questions, will help you to solve problems as they arise, increasing both your understanding and enjoyment of the whole training process.

BIBLIOGRAPHY

Introduction

Jesse Owens Quotes. (n.d.). BrainyQuote.com. Retrieved 13 December 2019, from Brainy-Quote.com Web site: https://www.brainy-quote.com/quotes/jesse_owens_166163

Scales, S. *Retriever Training* (Swan Hill, 1992).

Chapter 1

Coco Chanel Quotes. (n.d.). BrainyQuote.com. Retrieved December 13, 2019, from https://www.brainyquote.com/quotes/coco_chanel_119269

Dodds, J. and Laverdure, D. *Canine Nutrigenomics: The new science of feeding your dog for optimum health* (Dogwise Publishing, 2015).

Ericsson, A. and Pool, R. *Peak: Secrets from the new science of expertise* (Houghton Mifflin Harcourt, 2016).

Gladwell, M. *Outliers* (Penguin, 2009).

Lee, R *et al*. 'Chronic Corticosterone Exposure Increases Expression and Decreases Deoxyribonucleic Acid Methylation of *Fkbp5* in Mice', *Endocrinology* (September 2010, pp.4332–43).

Lin, X *et al*. 'Potential role of maternal lineage in the thoroughbred breeding strategy', *Reproduction, Fertility and Development* (May 2015, pp.1704–11).

Lush, J. *Animal Breeding Plans* (Iowa State College Press, 1937).

Macnamara, B. *et al*. 'The Relationship Between Deliberate Practice and Performance in Sports: A Meta-Analysis', *Perspectives on Psychological Science* (May 2016, pp.333–50)

Michelle Obama Quotes. (n.d.). BrainyQuote.com. Retrieved 13 December 2019, from https://www.brainyquote.com/quotes/michelle_obama_791420

Pele Quotes. (n.d.). BrainyQuote.com. Retrieved 13 December 2019, from https://www.brainy-quote.com/quotes/pele_737774

Riser, W. 'The dog as a model for the study of hip dysplasia: growth, form, and development of the normal and dysplastic hip joint', *Veterinary Pathology* (December 1975, pp.235–334).

Chapter 2

Armstrong, L. *It's not about the bike: My journey back to life* (Yellow Jersey Press, 2001).

McConnell, P. *For the Love of a Dog: Understanding emotion in you and your best friend* (Ballantine Books, 2007).

McGee, P. Self-Confidence: *The remarkable truth of why a small change can make a big difference* (2010).

Starkes, J and Erisson, A. *Expert Performance in Sports: Advances in Research on Sport Exercise* (Human Kinetics, 2003).

Chapter 3

Grandin, T. *Making animals happy: How to Create the Best Life for Pets and Other Animals* (Bloomsbury, 2009).

Panksepp, J. 'Affective Consciousness: Core Emotional Feelings in Animals and Humans', *Consciousness and Cognition* 14 (2005, pp.30–80).

Chapter 4

Breland, K. and Breland, M. 'A field of applied animal psychology', *American Psychologist*, (June 1951, pp.202–04).

Lucius Annaeus Seneca Quotes. (n.d.). BrainyQuote.com. Retrieved December 13, 2019, from https://www.brainyquote.com/quotes/lucius_annaeus_seneca_162971

Mech, D. 'Alpha Status, Dominance, and Division of Labor in Wolf Packs', *Canadian Journal of Zoology* (1999).

Pavlov, I. *The Work of the Digestive Glands* (1902).

Pryor, K. *Don't Shoot the Dog! The New Art of Teaching and Training* (Ringpress, 1984).

Rafkin, L. 'The Anti-Cesar Millan / Ian Dunbar's been succeeding for 25 years with lure-reward dog training; how come he's been usurped by the flashy, aggressive TV host?', *San Francisco Chronicle* (15 October 2006).

Sanderson, C. *The Practical Breaking and Training of Gundogs* (original 1922; Vintage Dog Books reprinted 2008).

Schenkel, R. 'Expression Studies on Wolves: Captivity Observations' (Zoological Institute of the University of Basle, 1947).

Skinner, B. *The Behaviour of Organisms* (D. Appleton & Company 1938).

Chapter 5

Fennell, J. *The Dog Listener: Learning the Language of your best friend* (2002).

Scales, S. *Retriever Training* (Swan Hill, 1992).

Chapter 7

Affenzeller, N. *et al.* 'Playful activity post-learning improves training performance in Labrador Retriever dogs (*Canis lupus familiaris*)', *Physiology & Behavior* (October 2016, pp.62–73).

Osborne, D. *et al.* 'The neuroenergetics of stress hormones in the hippocampus and implications for memory', *Frontiers in Neuroscience* (May 2015).

Seneca Quotes (n.d) GoodReads.com. Retrieved 13 December 2019, from www.goodreads. com/quotes/17490-luck-is-what-happens-when-preparation-meets-opportunity

Chapter 8

Coren, S. *Understanding Your Dog For Dummies* (For Dummies, 2013).

The Kennel Club. *Field Trial Regulations (including Gundog Working Tests)* (The Kennel Club, 2019).

Miller, H. *et al.* 'Object permanence in dogs: invisible displacement in a rotation task', *Psychonomic Bulletin & Review* (January 2009, pp.150–5).

Chapter 9

The Kennel Club. *Field Trial Regulations (including Gundog Working Tests)* (The Kennel Club, 2019).

Chapter 10

Christopher Columbus Quotes. (n.d.). BrainyQuote.com. Retrieved 13 December 2019, from https://www.brainyquote.com/quotes/christopher_columbus_387643

Chapter 11

Christian Dior Quotes. (n.d.). BrainyQuote.com. Retrieved 13 December 2019, from https://www.brainyquote.com/quotes/christian_dior_636666

Chapter 12

European Aviation Standards Authority 'The Principles of Threat and Error Management (TEM) for Helicopter Pilots, Instructors and Training Organisations' leaflet (December 2014).

Patty Berg Quotes. (n.d.). BrainyQuote.com. Retrieved 13 December 2019, from https://www.brainyquote.com/quotes/patty_berg_184059

INDEX

RELATED TITLES FROM CROWOOD

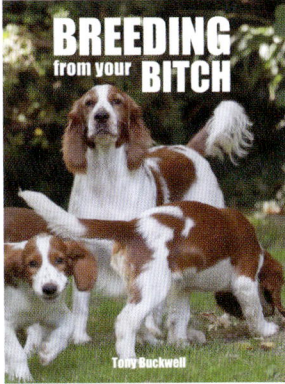

BREEDING from your BITCH
Tony Buckwell

978 1 78500 653 1

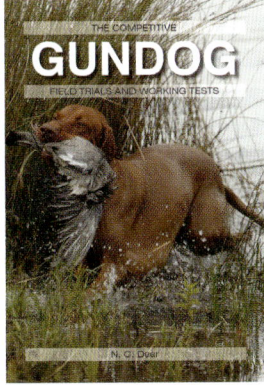

THE COMPETITIVE GUNDOG
FIELD TRIALS AND WORKING TESTS
N. C. Dear

978 1 84797 282 8

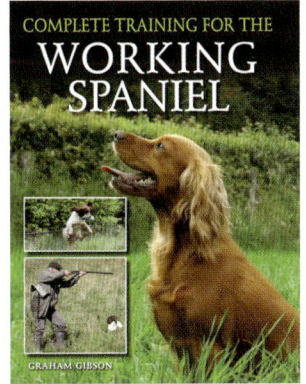

COMPLETE TRAINING FOR THE WORKING SPANIEL
GRAHAM GIBSON

978 1 84797 945 2

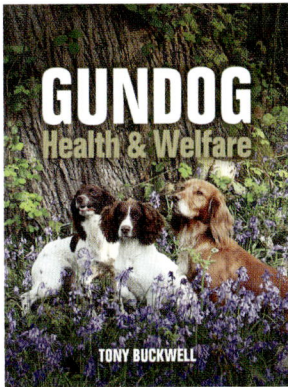

GUNDOG Health & Welfare
TONY BUCKWELL

978 1 78500 387 5

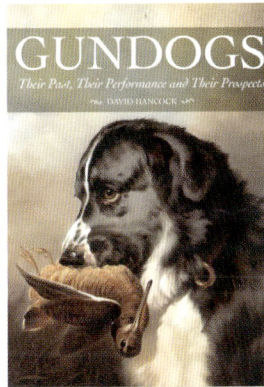

GUNDOGS
Their Past, Their Performance and Their Prospects
DAVID HANCOCK

978 1 84797 492 1

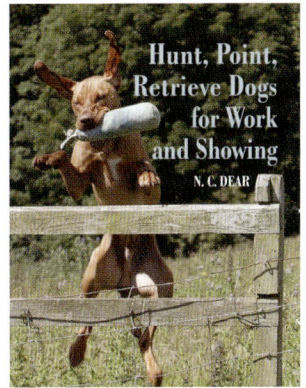

Hunt, Point, Retrieve Dogs for Work and Showing
N. C. DEAR

978 1 84797 082 4

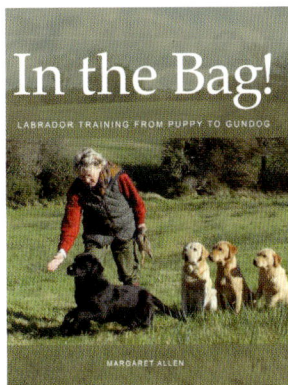

In the Bag!
LABRADOR TRAINING FROM PUPPY TO GUNDOG
MARGARET ALLEN

978 1 84797 481 5

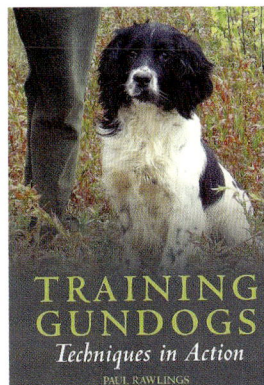

TRAINING GUNDOGS
Techniques in Action
PAUL RAWLINGS

978 1 86126 984 3

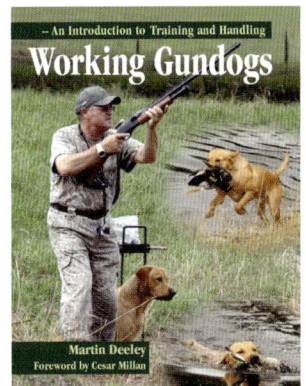

Working Gundogs
– An Introduction to Training and Handling
Martin Deeley
Foreword by Cesar Millan

978 1 84797 099 2